Chrysalis Debt

Chrysalis Debt

Matthew Petchinsky

1

Chrysalis Debt: Reborn into Wealth

By: Matthew Petchinsky

Disclaimer

This book is intended for educational and informational purposes only. *Chrysalis Debt: Reborn into Wealth* explores the psychological, behavioral, strategic, and practical aspects of transforming one's relationship with debt and money. It does not constitute financial, legal, tax, accounting, investment, medical, or psychological advice. The strategies, examples, case studies, metaphors, and frameworks presented are provided as general guidance and personal development tools, and may not be suitable for every individual or financial situation.

The author is not acting as a licensed financial advisor, certified public accountant, attorney, credit counselor, investment broker, therapist, or fiduciary. Readers are strongly encouraged to consult qualified professionals before making any significant financial decisions, including but not limited to debt restructuring, bankruptcy filings, loan consolidation, investment strategies, business formation, tax planning, credit repair, or asset protection planning. Financial laws, tax regulations, lending practices, and credit reporting standards vary by jurisdiction and change over time. It is the reader's responsibility to verify current laws and regulations applicable to their location and personal circumstances.

All income examples, debt elimination scenarios, wealth-building projections, and financial transformations discussed in this book are illustrative only. They are not guarantees or promises of specific results. Individual outcomes depend on numerous factors including income level, discipline, market conditions, access to capital, credit history, economic climate, timing, skill, health, opportunity, and personal decision-making. Past results do not guarantee future outcomes. Wealth creation involves risk, and there is always the possibility of financial loss.

Discussions surrounding credit systems, lending structures, consumer finance, and economic models are presented for educational reflection and strategic understanding. Nothing in this book should be interpreted as encouragement to evade lawful financial obligations, manipulate financial institutions illegally, misrepresent income, commit fraud, avoid taxes, or engage in deceptive or unethical conduct. The author explicitly condemns illegal financial activity. Ethical integrity and lawful compliance are foundational to sustainable wealth creation.

This book may include psychological reframing techniques, mindset shifts, behavioral exercises, journaling prompts, and identity transformation frameworks designed to support emotional healing around money and debt. These practices are not a substitute for professional mental health treatment. Readers experiencing severe financial anxiety, depression, compulsive spending, gambling addiction, trauma, or crisis-level distress should seek licensed therapeutic or counseling support.

Business concepts and entrepreneurial strategies presented herein carry inherent risk. Starting or scaling a business may involve financial loss, legal exposure, taxation complexities, market volatility, and operational challenges. The reader assumes full responsibility for evaluating risks and performing appropriate due diligence before implementing any business model or income strategy discussed in this book.

References to financial tools, platforms, banking systems, credit instruments, or economic mechanisms are not endorsements, sponsorships, or affiliations unless explicitly stated. The author receives no guaranteed compensation for the reader's financial decisions and assumes no liability for outcomes resulting from the application of this material.

By reading this book, you acknowledge that you are solely responsible for your financial choices, actions, and results. You agree that the author and publisher shall not be held liable for any loss, damages, liabilities, claims, or expenses incurred directly or indirectly from the use or misuse of the information provided.

Chrysalis Debt: Reborn into Wealth is ultimately a transformational framework—a metaphorical chrysalis through which readers are invited to evolve their relationship with debt, money, and self-worth. The transformation, however, is yours alone to enact, guided by wisdom, discipline, lawful conduct, and informed decision-making.

Introduction: Wealth Isn't Created — It's Remembered

There is a version of you that has never feared money.

Not because that version inherited riches.
Not because luck smiled.
Not because the system was kind.

But because that version never forgot who they were.

Chrysalis Debt: Reborn into Wealth begins from a radical premise: wealth is not something you construct from nothing — it is something you recover from distortion. Scarcity is learned. Debt loops are patterned. Financial ruin is often karmic repetition disguised as circumstance. And what has been patterned can be dissolved.

This book is not about budgeting tricks alone.
It is about energetic identity collapse.
It is about frequency realignment.
It is about the Death Moth.

The Debt Isn't Just Financial

Most people believe debt is a math problem.
Interest rates. Minimum payments. Credit scores.
Numbers rising and falling like tides.

But beneath the numbers is something older.

Inherited poverty scripts.
Family trauma around survival.
Shame coded into nervous systems.
Generational beliefs such as:

- "Money is hard."
- "People like us never get ahead."
- "If I have more, someone else must have less."
- "Wealth corrupts."
- "Security requires suffering."

These are not financial facts. They are psychic imprints.

Debt often repeats through families not because of intelligence deficits, but because of frequency inheritance. The body learns scarcity before the mind ever sees a credit card. And by adulthood, that scarcity feels normal — familiar — almost safe.

But what if financial collapse is not a curse...
but a cocoon?

The Death Moth Frequency

The Death Moth is not destruction for chaos.
It is destruction for transformation.

In nature, the moth is drawn to flame — not to die, but to navigate through light. In this book, Death Moth frequency represents a transmutational current: the energetic pattern that disintegrates false structures so something truer can emerge.

Debt feels like rot.
Like decay.
Like endings.

And yet decay feeds soil.

The Death Moth frequency is the willingness to enter financial shadow without denial. To let illusions burn. To allow outdated identities — "the struggler," "the debtor," "the broke creative," "the underdog" — to dissolve in sacred combustion.

You do not channel Death Moth frequency to escape debt.

You channel it to metabolize it.

To turn karmic ruin into nutrient.

Chrysalis as Financial Metamorphosis

A chrysalis does not decorate the caterpillar.
It dissolves it.

Inside the cocoon, the caterpillar's body breaks down into imaginal cells — blueprints of the butterfly. Those imaginal cells already contain the design of wings.

Likewise, wealth is not built from scratch.
It is encoded.

Within every financial breakdown is an imaginal blueprint — a higher earning capacity, a strategic intelligence, a disciplined operator, an intuitive wealth architect. But that identity cannot emerge while clinging to the old form.

Chrysalis Debt is about allowing financial identity death.

The version of you that overspends for comfort.
The version that undercharges from guilt.
The version that fears visibility.
The version that sabotages growth to stay familiar.

These identities are not evil. They were protective.

But protection becomes prison when it overstays.

Shedding the Inherited Poverty-Mindset

Many readers carry inherited scripts that were never consciously chosen.

Scarcity loops such as:

- Earning more, then creating emergencies.
- Paying off debt, then re-entering it.
- Receiving opportunity, then hesitating.
- Saving money, then feeling unsafe.

These loops are not random. They are nervous system echoes.

Chrysalis Debt introduces wealth reprogramming not as positive thinking, but as cellular rewriting. Through structured reflection, energetic recalibration, strategic implementation, and transmutation rituals, you will:

- Identify inherited financial patterns.
- Interrupt karmic debt cycles.
- Collapse scarcity identity.
- Rebuild wealth architecture from a sovereign center.

This is not magical escapism.
It is disciplined transformation.

Rituals in this book are symbolic neural interventions. They anchor intention into action. They convert shame into strategy. They shift self-concept so behavior can follow.

Wealth does not enter a system that still believes it is unsafe.

Karmic Financial Ruin as Seed

Financial collapse can feel humiliating.
Credit damage can feel permanent.
Failure can feel defining.

But in soil science, controlled burn increases fertility.

When illusions about money burn away — fantasies of quick rescue, dependence on unstable systems, avoidance of responsibility — something clearer emerges.

Precision.
Ownership.
Sovereignty.

The Death Moth frequency teaches you to stop identifying with the ashes.

You are not your debt.

You are the one who survived it.

And survival contains data.

Within every financial mistake is encoded intelligence:

- Lessons about leverage.
- Lessons about discipline.
- Lessons about boundaries.
- Lessons about valuation.
- Lessons about timing.

The seed of infinite wealth is not optimism.

It is awareness.

Infinite Wealth Defined

Infinite wealth does not mean infinite cash in a vault.

It means:

- Infinite capacity to generate value.
- Infinite creativity.
- Infinite resilience.
- Infinite recalibration ability.
- Infinite ownership of your earning identity.

Money flows toward value creation and stability.

When you remember who you are — a generator, not a beggar; a builder, not a victim — wealth becomes a byproduct of identity alignment.

You stop chasing money.
You become magnetic to it.

Not through fantasy — but through structure.

This Book Is a Threshold

You are not reading this by accident.

If you are here, something has already begun dissolving.

Perhaps:

- You are tired of repeating cycles.
- You sense you are capable of more.
- You feel financial shame that no longer fits.
- You are ready to stop blaming systems and start mastering strategy.
- You want wealth without spiritual compromise.

Chrysalis Debt does not deny the existence of flawed economic structures. It does not romanticize struggle. It does not pretend that markets are equal.

But it insists on one uncompromising truth:

Your internal architecture determines how you move within any system.

When scarcity dissolves, strategy sharpens.
When shame dissolves, negotiation strengthens.
When identity upgrades, income follows.

The Invitation

This is your cocoon phase.
It may feel uncomfortable.
It may challenge long-held beliefs.
It may confront you with habits you justified.
But you are not here to be comfortable.
You are here to remember.
The Death Moth does not fear flame.
It understands transformation requires heat.
Let the old identity burn.
Let inherited poverty scripts collapse.
Let karmic debt loops disintegrate.
Inside you is imaginal wealth architecture.
You do not have to create it.
You only have to remember it.

Chapter One – Molting the Poverty Shell

The Shell Was Protection, Not Identity

The poverty shell did not form because you were weak. It formed because you adapted. At some point in your life—perhaps in childhood, perhaps during a season of financial collapse—your nervous system learned that money was unstable, unpredictable, or dangerous. The shell became armor. Armor becomes habit. Habit becomes identity.

Scarcity thinking is rarely conscious. It hides inside phrases like "I can't afford that," even when the real truth is "I am afraid to expand." It whispers that safety is found in contraction. It confuses frugality with fear. It blurs discipline with deprivation.

Energetically, the poverty shell feels dense. It tightens the chest when discussing income. It produces shame when checking bank balances. It creates subtle guilt when receiving more than you once had. That density is not moral failure. It is stored memory.

Psychologically, the shell reinforces patterns of self-limitation. You may downplay ambition to avoid disappointment. You may overwork to compensate for insecurity. You may reject opportunity because visibility feels unsafe. These are not flaws; they are trauma responses wearing financial clothing.

Molting begins when you stop condemning the shell and start understanding it. You do not rip armor off violently. You soften it. You outgrow it. You let it fall away when it no longer serves survival.

Identifying the Trauma Imprint

Money trauma often forms before your first paycheck. It forms in overheard arguments about bills. It forms when caregivers express fear about rent. It forms when abundance is followed by loss. The nervous system records these moments as warnings.

Trauma imprints operate through repetition. If money once disappeared suddenly, you may expect it to disappear again. If you were criticized for wanting more, ambition may feel selfish. If financial instability created chaos, wealth may feel destabilizing.

Energetically, trauma imprints create contraction loops. When income rises, anxiety rises with it. When opportunities appear, suspicion follows. When debt shrinks, a subconscious voice anticipates disaster. These loops keep the shell intact.

Psychologically, trauma imprints distort perception. You may misread neutral events as threats. You may assume scarcity even when numbers improve. You may sabotage growth to maintain emotional familiarity.

Awareness dissolves distortion. When you name the imprint, you remove its invisibility. When you see the pattern, you interrupt automation. Molting begins with observation free from shame.

Scarcity as a Nervous System Habit

Scarcity is not always about income level. It is about regulation. Two individuals can earn the same amount; one feels secure, the other perpetually endangered. The difference often lies in nervous system conditioning.

A dysregulated system equates expansion with risk. More clients means more responsibility. Higher income means higher expectations. Visibility means vulnerability. The body resists growth because it interprets it as threat.

Scarcity habits manifest subtly. You may hesitate to invest in tools that expand you. You may delay raising prices. You may cling to outdated strategies because familiarity feels safer than innovation.

Energetically, scarcity narrows possibility. It shrinks vision. It lowers tolerance for delayed gratification. It keeps focus on immediate survival rather than long-term architecture.

To molt, you must teach your nervous system that stability can coexist with expansion. Regulation precedes wealth. Calm precedes clarity. Security must be internal before it can be sustained externally.

Rewriting the Financial Self-Concept

Identity governs behavior more powerfully than goals. If you identify as "someone who struggles," you will unconsciously recreate struggle. If you identify as "bad with money," your decisions will align with that belief.

Self-concept is constructed from memory, repetition, and narrative. You may have told yourself the same financial story for years. "I never get ahead." "Money slips through my fingers." "I always start over." Repetition makes fiction feel factual.

Energetically, identity functions like a broadcast signal. It influences how you negotiate, how you price, how you invest, and how you plan. You do not need mystical belief to recognize this—confidence alone alters financial outcomes.

Rewriting self-concept requires evidence. Small financial wins matter. Tracking progress matters. Honoring discipline matters. Identity shifts when behavior proves new capacity.

Molting the poverty shell means stepping into the identity of someone who builds, maintains, and multiplies value. Not someone lucky. Not someone rescued. Someone responsible and sovereign.

Grieving the Old Narrative

Molting involves loss. You may lose the comfort of blaming circumstances. You may lose the identity of the underdog. You may lose the familiar rhythm of crisis and recovery.

Grief surfaces when growth demands accountability. It can feel easier to remain the struggler than to become the architect. The struggler receives sympathy. The architect carries responsibility.

Energetically, grief is part of transformation. It signals that an identity is dissolving. It does not mean you are regressing. It means you are shedding.

Psychologically, allowing grief prevents self-sabotage. If you suppress it, you may recreate struggle just to return to familiarity. If you process it, you move forward cleanly.

Honor the shell for protecting you. Then release it. Gratitude accelerates transformation more effectively than resentment ever could.

Stabilizing Before Expanding

Before increasing income, stabilize behavior. Before multiplying wealth, secure foundations. Expansion without stability recreates chaos.

Stability means clear tracking. It means knowing your numbers without emotional collapse. It means separating worth from net worth. It means making decisions from clarity rather than panic.

Energetically, stability feels grounded. It feels slower but stronger. It resists impulsive spending and impulsive investing alike. It prioritizes long-term architecture over short-term dopamine.

Psychologically, stability builds trust with yourself. When you keep small financial promises—tracking expenses, honoring budgets, saving consistently—you teach your mind that growth is safe.

Molting the poverty shell is not dramatic. It is methodical. It is disciplined. It is daily.

Financial Tip: Track Without Emotion

Begin tracking every dollar that enters and exits your life for 30 days. Do not judge. Do not justify. Simply observe patterns. Emotional neutrality is key; this is data, not morality.

Create categories that reflect reality rather than aspiration. If spending on convenience is high, label it clearly. If income fluctuates, record the rhythm. Precision dissolves denial.

At the end of 30 days, review patterns calmly. Identify one leakage point to correct. Sustainable wealth begins with accurate awareness.

Exercises

Exercise: Trauma Mapping

Step 1: Write down your earliest memory involving money stress.
Step 2: Identify the emotion you felt in that moment.
Step 3: Note any beliefs formed (e.g., "Money disappears").
Step 4: Reflect on how that belief influences current behavior.
Step 5: Rewrite the belief into a grounded alternative ("Money requires structure, and I can build structure").

Exercise: Scarcity Loop Interruption

Step 1: Identify a recurring financial pattern.

Step 2: Trace the emotional trigger preceding it.

Step 3: Create a pause ritual—24 hours before financial decisions.

Step 4: During the pause, review numbers objectively.

Step 5: Make the decision from logic rather than emotion.

Exercise: Identity Upgrade Declaration

Step 1: Write your current financial identity in one sentence.
Step 2: Write the identity you are stepping into.
Step 3: List three behaviors aligned with the new identity.
Step 4: Implement one behavior immediately.
Step 5: Track consistency for 21 days.

Financial Ideas

Skill Monetization Expansion

Audit existing skills and identify under-leveraged value. Many individuals possess expertise they undervalue due to familiarity. What feels ordinary to you may be high-value to others.

Research market rates for comparable skills. Underpricing often reflects self-concept, not market demand. Correct pricing aligns identity with value.

Create one additional revenue stream from an existing skill before pursuing entirely new ventures. Expansion from stability accelerates growth.

Debt Reframing Strategy

List all debts clearly with balances and interest rates. Replace emotional language with neutral description. Debt is data.

Prioritize either highest interest rate (avalanche method) or smallest balance (snowball method) depending on psychological need for momentum. Choose consciously.

Celebrate each reduction milestone. Momentum reinforces identity transformation.

Emergency Buffer Creation

Begin building a small emergency fund, even if modest. The amount matters less than the habit.

Automate contributions weekly. Consistency matters more than size. Stability reduces nervous system threat response.

As the buffer grows, anxiety decreases. Calm creates space for strategic thinking rather than reactive survival.

Journal Prompts

1. What was my earliest money memory?
2. What belief about wealth did I inherit?
3. Where do I feel financial anxiety in my body?
4. What identity have I outgrown?
5. How has struggle served me?
6. What does stability feel like?
7. What behavior reinforces scarcity?
8. What small financial win can I create this week?
9. Who would I be without money shame?
10. What does financial sovereignty mean to me?

Closing Reflection

Molting is not glamorous. It is quiet. It is uncomfortable. It requires patience.

The poverty shell once protected you. Honor it. But recognize that what once shielded you now limits you. Wealth begins not with external accumulation but internal stabilization.

You are not broken. You are transforming.

Let the old identity fall away naturally.

Stability first. Expansion second.
Sovereignty always.

Chapter Two – The Debt Sigil Equation

Debt as Contained Power

Debt is rarely neutral in the psyche. It carries emotion, memory, and projection. Shame attaches to it. Fear amplifies it. Avoidance feeds it. Yet beneath the emotional charge lies something structurally neutral: obligation plus time.

Energy follows attention. When debt is viewed as an enemy, it becomes a psychic predator. When it is viewed as a teacher, it becomes instruction. When it is viewed as raw power awaiting direction, it becomes convertible.

The Debt Sigil Equation begins with a radical shift: debt is compressed life force. It represents value already accessed. It represents trust extended by a system. It represents capacity exercised prematurely.

Energetically, debt is forward momentum misaligned with structure. It is expansion without anchoring. The equation does not deny repayment responsibility. It reframes the energetic field surrounding it so the "debt charge" becomes usable fuel.

When you convert shame into strategy, debt stops draining and begins instructing. Power returns to the operator—meaning **you**.

The Sigil as a Reprogramming Device

A sigil is a symbolic compression of intention. It bypasses surface resistance and speaks directly to the subconscious. Whether you treat it as magick, psychology, or sacred symbolism, it functions as a **bridge between will and behavior**.

In financial transformation, a sigil becomes a visual contract. It anchors identity shift. It turns vague goals into a repeatable point of focus. Most people lose momentum because their intention stays abstract; sigils make intention visible.

The Debt Sigil Equation is a structure you can return to daily:

Debt (D) × Discipline (Δ) + Direction (→) = Prosperity (P)

Your sigil will embody this formula. It will remind your nervous system that debt can be converted through disciplined action, not avoided through fear.

This is not about "wishing." This is about **binding focus**.

Moth-Binding Magick: Conversion, Not Escape

The moth represents attraction to light. Moth-binding is not trapping it—it is **aligning it**. You are binding your attention to illumination rather than chaos, to structured flame rather than self-destructive burn.

Debt energy scatters when avoided. It intensifies when obsessed over emotionally. Moth-binding centers it. You bind your attention to repayment strategy, prosperity habits, and wealth creation discipline.

Energetically, binding prevents leakage. It stops you from bleeding power through panic-spending, denial, or self-hatred. It keeps your focus anchored to action.

Psychologically, moth-binding reduces avoidance behavior. Instead of fearing the balance, you ritualize engagement with it. Engagement builds authority.

The moth does not die in flame when guided properly. It navigates by it.

Breaking Shame and Claiming Authority

Shame keeps debt alive longer than interest rates. Shame encourages secrecy. Secrecy prevents planning. Lack of planning prolongs the cycle. The longer the cycle runs, the more your identity fuses with it.

Authority breaks the cycle. Authority means you stop acting like debt is a monster and start treating it like data plus discipline. Authority does not mean arrogance. It means *ownership without collapse.*

Energetically, authority changes your posture. It changes your voice when you negotiate. It changes your decisions when you price your work. Prosperity follows that stability.

Psychologically, ritualized authority dissolves learned helplessness. When you perform structured actions repeatedly, your brain starts believing: "I am capable. I can handle this. I can build."

Debt does not shrink through self-punishment. It shrinks through structured power.

The Equation as Daily Architecture

The Debt Sigil Equation is not a poem—it's a blueprint. It works because it translates emotional chaos into repeatable structure.

Debt multiplied by discipline means: automatic payments, planned spending, controlled leakage, consistent tracking. Direction means: intentional income expansion, learning valuable skills, and building multiple streams slowly.

Prosperity emerges as **both** reduced liability and increased capacity. It is subtraction and addition at the same time. Your life becomes lighter while your earning identity becomes stronger.

This chapter makes the transformation tangible. You will create a sigil, bind it to action, and turn debt into a tool rather than a terror.

Conversion is not dramatic.

Conversion is consistent.

Prosperity as Structured Flame

Flame without containment destroys. Flame inside a forge builds. Prosperity is structured flame—disciplined heat used for creation.

If you try to "manifest" without structure, you burn yourself out. If you use structure without belief, you become rigid and joyless. This system fuses both: symbolic ignition and strategic scaffolding.

Energetically, prosperity feels calm, not frantic. It grows from architecture, not adrenaline. It scales from routine, not desperation.

Psychologically, this stability builds confidence. You stop fearing fluctuations because you understand how to adjust. You stop collapsing because you have a system.

The moth no longer spirals.

It orbits light with intention.

Financial Tip: Automate Discipline First

Automation removes emotional friction. When discipline is automated, your nervous system doesn't have to "decide" to be responsible every month—it simply happens. That one shift eliminates a large portion of avoidance.

Step into authority by setting automatic minimum payments for every debt. Then add a second automated payment—even small—toward the debt you're attacking first. This separates survival maintenance from transformation momentum.

Review your automation monthly, not daily. Daily checking often triggers anxiety spirals; monthly review keeps you engaged without obsession. Let structure carry your progress while your mind focuses on income-building and identity growth.

Ritual – The Debt Sigil Binding Rite

Materials Needed:

Black candle (transformation), gold candle (prosperity), paper, pen, fireproof dish, salt, small bowl of water.

Steps:

Step 1: Clear a surface and place the black candle on your left and the gold candle on your right. Put the bowl of water in front of you and sprinkle a line of salt around your workspace.
Step 2: On the paper, write your **total debt number** at the top. Under it, write the equation: **D** × **Δ** + → = **P**.
Step 3: Create your sigil by combining the letters **D, Δ, →, P** into a single symbol. Simplify it until it feels clean and "final."
Step 4: Light the black candle and say: "I release the shame and distortion around debt."
Step 5: Light the gold candle and say: "I claim disciplined conversion and prosperity."
Step 6: Hold the paper with both hands and visualize your debt as dark static compressing into a dense sphere. See that sphere becoming fuel instead of fear.
Step 7: Fold the paper three times toward you (to draw power in).
Step 8: Place the paper in the fireproof dish and burn it safely.
Step 9: As it burns, speak: "Debt multiplied by discipline, guided by direction, becomes prosperity. My focus is bound to structured flame."
Step 10: Dip your fingertips into the salted water and touch your forehead and chest (symbolizing clarity and steadiness).
Step 11: Let the candles burn for a few minutes, then extinguish them (do not blow if you prefer symbolic containment—snuffing is fine).
Step 12: End by writing one action you will complete within 24 hours to prove the binding is real.

Spell 1 – Moth of Focus Spell

Materials Needed: White candle, small mirror, notebook, pen.

Steps:

Step 1: Light the white candle and place it so the flame reflects in the mirror.

Step 2: In your notebook, write ONE action you will complete in the next 48 hours (example: "Call creditor," "Set automatic payment," "List one product/service for sale").

Step 3: Place your palm over the notebook and breathe slowly for 10 breaths.

Step 4: Look into the mirror and speak the incantation clearly:

"Like moth to light, my focus is bound. I do not scatter. I do not delay. I move with disciplined fire."

Step 5: Close the notebook and place it under the mirror until the action is completed.

Step 6: When you complete the action, return and extinguish the candle as a seal.

Spell 2 – Prosperity Multiplication Spell

Materials Needed: Green candle, coin, string or thread.

Steps:

Step 1: Tie the string around the coin in a simple loop.

Step 2: Light the green candle and hold the coin near (not in) the flame.

Step 3: Visualize three streams of income forming like golden threads—small, stable, consistent.

Step 4: Speak the incantation:

"From compressed energy, wealth expands. From obligation, opportunity rises. From discipline, prosperity multiplies."

Step 5: Wrap the string three times around your fingers and feel the "binding" of consistency.

Step 6: Place the coin somewhere you touch daily (wallet, desk, planner) as a reminder that multiplication is built through repetition.

Step 7: Each time you touch it, take one small action that supports income or debt payoff.

Spell 3 – Discipline Anchor Spell

Materials Needed: Small stone, black marker.

Steps:

Step 1: Draw your Debt Sigil on the stone.

Step 2: Hold the stone firmly and breathe in for 4 counts, hold for 4, exhale for 6. Repeat 3 times.

Step 3: Speak the incantation:

"I am consistent. I am precise. I am sovereign. My discipline is anchored and my wealth is inevitable."

Step 4: Place the stone where you do money tasks (near laptop, ledger, bills, or planner).

Step 5: Touch it before any financial action to signal your nervous system: "I am safe to be responsible."

Exercises

Exercise 1 – Debt Visibility Without Collapse

Step 1: Write every debt on one page: creditor, balance, interest rate, minimum payment.
Step 2: Add a "due date" column.
Step 3: Circle the highest interest rate.
Step 4: Star the smallest balance.
Step 5: Choose whether you will attack by avalanche (highest interest) or snowball (smallest balance).
Step 6: Write one sentence: "My plan is _______ and I commit for 90 days."

Exercise 2 – Conversion Plan Blueprint

Step 1: Choose your target debt.
Step 2: Decide your extra monthly payment amount (even $10 counts).
Step 3: Identify one expense to reduce or replace to fund it.
Step 4: Set an automatic transfer/payment for that extra amount.
Step 5: Write your 90-day target in a single measurable line.
Step 6: Put a weekly reminder to check progress once—no spiraling.

Exercise 3 – Income Signal Upgrade

Step 1: List 5 skills you already have (writing, design, editing, coaching, research, selling, organizing).
Step 2: Circle the skill people have praised or paid you for before.
Step 3: Pick one "offer" you can create in 7 days from that skill.
Step 4: Write the simplest version of it (minimum viable offer).
Step 5: Set a price and a delivery method.
Step 6: Promote it to 3 places or 3 people within 72 hours.

Financial Ideas

Debt-to-Offer Alchemy

Debt often formed because you needed something: relief, stability, tools, survival. Instead of viewing that as failure, treat it as data about what you value and what you require to function. That data can be converted into an offer that serves others.

Look at what your debt funded—education, devices, transportation, household needs, emergencies. Ask: what skill did I develop or what problem did I survive because of this? Prosperity grows when survival lessons become value.

Build a small, clear product or service that directly converts your lived experience into usefulness. When debt becomes the seed of an offer, it stops being "just loss" and becomes a catalyst.

Micro-Stream Layering for Stability

Instead of chasing one massive breakthrough, create three small income layers: one dependable, one flexible, one growth-based. Stability reduces nervous system panic and increases your ability to plan.

A dependable layer might be consistent sales or steady services. A flexible layer might be one-off gigs or small products. A growth layer might be something scalable like digital products or long-form content.

The goal is not to overwhelm yourself. The goal is to stop treating money as one fragile pipe. Multiple pipes reduce fear—and fear reduction is a prosperity multiplier.

Interest-Rate Negotiation + Structure Upgrade

Many people never ask for reduced interest or better terms because shame makes them avoid contact. But negotiation is not begging—it's strategy. Even a small reduction can cut payoff time dramatically.

Call your creditors, ask about hardship programs, reduced APR, or payment arrangements. You are not promising what you cannot deliver; you are requesting structured terms you can honor consistently.

After negotiation, reinforce structure: automate payments, schedule review dates, and avoid daily checking. Prosperity grows when your relationship with debt becomes organized rather than emotional.

Meditation – Structured Flame Conversion (Step-by-step)

Step 1: Sit upright with both feet on the floor. Place one hand on your chest and one on your lower abdomen.

Step 2: Inhale slowly for 4 counts, hold for 2, exhale for 6. Repeat this cycle 10 times.

Step 3: Visualize your debt as a dark cloud in front of you—dense but contained.

Step 4: Imagine a golden ring forming around it labeled **Discipline**.

Step 5: Imagine a clear arrow forming from your heart to the cloud labeled **Direction**.

Step 6: Watch the dark cloud compress into a small sphere, then begin to glow—turning from dark into gold.

Step 7: Repeat silently for 3 minutes: "I convert. I structure. I multiply."

Step 8: Ask yourself: "What is the next right financial action?"

Step 9: Let the answer arrive without forcing it.

Step 10: Open your eyes and write down the one action you will complete today.

Journal Prompts

1. What part of me feels ashamed about debt, and what does it fear would happen if others knew?
2. Where do I avoid money tasks, and what emotion is underneath the avoidance?
3. What does "discipline" mean to me when it's loving instead of punishing?
4. What would change if I treated debt as data instead of a sentence?
5. What is my biggest scarcity trigger, and what is a healthier response?
6. What action proves I'm no longer powerless with money?
7. What is one income stream I can build from a skill I already have?
8. What does "structured flame" look like in my daily choices?
9. What's the most realistic 90-day debt goal I can commit to?
10. Who am I becoming as I convert debt into prosperity?

Closing Reflection

The Debt Sigil Equation is a covenant between your future and your present. It is the point where shame stops driving and structure takes the wheel.

You are not here to escape responsibility. You are here to **convert it**. Debt becomes fuel when you bind focus, automate discipline, and apply direction consistently.

Let this be the chapter where you stop flinching.
Where you look directly at the numbers without collapse.
Where you turn obligation into architecture.

The moth does not burn when it is guided.
It becomes a navigator of light.

Chapter Three – Burn the Ledger

The Inherited Ledger

Before you ever opened your first bank account, a ledger was already written for you. Not in ink, but in attitude. Not in numbers, but in nervous system responses. Every family carries a financial mythology—stories about who prospers, who struggles, who "deserves," and who must sacrifice.

Some lineages normalize debt as survival. Others glorify suffering as virtue. Some worship wealth yet fear it simultaneously. These contradictions form invisible scripts that guide behavior long before conscious choice enters the room.

Ancestral financial curses are rarely mystical punishments. They are repeated patterns. Bankruptcy across generations. Underearning despite talent. Overspending after moments of abundance. Avoidance of negotiation. Fear of visibility.

When these patterns are not examined, they masquerade as personality traits. "I'm just bad with money." "People like us don't get ahead." These phrases are echoes, not truths.

Burning the ledger means refusing to carry forward what was never yours to begin with.

The Myth of Predetermined Scarcity

Many people secretly believe that wealth is allocated to others. That prosperity is a limited inheritance distributed unevenly at birth. This belief is reinforced by lived experience, systemic realities, and family narratives.

Yet scarcity myths often operate internally even when external circumstances change. You may earn more but still expect collapse. You may save money yet anticipate loss. You may succeed but prepare for punishment.

The myth of predetermined scarcity keeps you loyal to struggle. Loyalty to struggle can feel like loyalty to family. Breaking patterns can feel like betrayal. This emotional complexity is why change requires ritual, not just strategy.

Ritual marks transition. It signals to the psyche: something old is ending. Without ceremony, the subconscious clings to familiarity.

The ledger must be burned symbolically before it can be dissolved behaviorally.

Fire as Cleansing Structure

Fire has always represented transformation. It destroys, but it also purifies. It breaks down material so it can reconfigure into something new. Fire in this chapter represents decisive release.

Financial incineration does not mean ignoring debts or responsibilities. It means burning inherited shame, inherited fear, inherited resignation. It means separating obligation from identity.

Energetically, fire signals finality. When something is burned, it cannot be returned to its former form. Ash does not reassemble into paper.

Psychologically, symbolic destruction disrupts internal repetition. It creates a rupture in the script. That rupture becomes an opening.

Burning the ledger is not about erasing reality. It is about rewriting authority.

From Curse to Contract

Ancestral financial patterns feel like curses because they are unconscious contracts. You may feel obligated to struggle because others did. You may fear surpassing relatives financially. You may self-sabotage to remain emotionally aligned with your origin story.

Burning the ledger severs unconscious contracts. It does not reject your lineage. It releases inherited limits.

Transformation requires grief. You may feel sadness recognizing how long these patterns persisted. You may feel anger. You may feel guilt. All are part of release.

When contracts dissolve, space opens. In that space, you can consciously design a new agreement with wealth.

Prosperity is not betrayal. It is evolution.

Ash as Fertile Ground

After incineration, ash remains. Ash is not waste. In soil science, ash enriches ground when integrated properly. Likewise, ancestral experience contains wisdom even if patterns were limiting.

You do not reject the resilience of those before you. You refine it. You honor survival while choosing expansion.

Energetically, ash represents neutralized charge. The emotional intensity around money begins to soften. Panic becomes planning. Shame becomes data.

Psychologically, ash allows reconstruction. When emotional fire subsides, strategic clarity becomes possible.

Burning the ledger clears ground so new architecture can rise.

The Sovereign Ledger

After release, you write a new ledger. Not one dictated by fear, but one structured by clarity. The sovereign ledger includes income goals, savings plans, debt reduction timelines, and growth strategies grounded in agency.

This ledger is not rigid dogma. It is responsive architecture. It adjusts with evidence. It evolves with growth.

Energetically, sovereignty feels steady. It does not spike with highs or crash with lows. It expands slowly and sustainably.

Psychologically, sovereignty reinforces identity. You no longer feel like a victim of financial weather. You become the architect of climate.

The old ledger burns. The new one begins.

Financial Tip: Separate Identity from Numbers

When reviewing finances, write two columns: "Facts" and "Stories." In the Facts column, record only numbers—balances, payments, income. In the Stories column, record emotional reactions and narratives.

This separation prevents numbers from morphing into self-judgment. A balance is not a verdict. It is a measurement. Measurements guide action; they do not define worth.

Practice this separation monthly. Over time, emotional charge decreases and strategic thinking strengthens. Authority replaces anxiety.

Ritual – The Ledger Incineration Rite

Materials Needed:

Paper, pen, fireproof dish, black candle, white candle, bowl of water.

Steps:

Step 1: On the paper, write all inherited money beliefs you recognize (examples: "Money is scarce," "We always struggle," "Debt is permanent").
Step 2: Light the black candle and say: "I acknowledge the inherited patterns."
Step 3: Read each belief aloud. After reading each one, say: "This pattern ends with me."
Step 4: Light the white candle and say: "I claim clarity and sovereignty."
Step 5: Fold the paper once away from you (symbolizing release).
Step 6: Place the paper in the fireproof dish and safely ignite it.
Step 7: As it burns, say: "I release inherited scarcity. I dissolve unconscious contracts. I am financially sovereign."
Step 8: Let the paper burn fully into ash.
Step 9: Dip fingers in water and touch forehead and chest, grounding yourself.
Step 10: Write one new belief that replaces the burned ones. Keep it visible for 30 days.

Spell 1 – Ancestral Release Spell

Materials Needed: White candle, small bowl of salt.

Steps:

Step 1: Light the candle.

Step 2: Place both hands over the bowl of salt.

Step 3: Speak:

"What was carried unconsciously is now made conscious. What was repeated without choice is now released."

Step 4: Visualize chains dissolving.

Step 5: Sprinkle a pinch of salt into running water (sink) to symbolize dissolution.

Spell 2 – Prosperity Lineage Spell

Materials Needed: Green candle, small notebook.

Steps:

Step 1: Light the green candle.

Step 2: Write three financial achievements you will create within 12 months.

Step 3: Speak:

"I honor the past and expand beyond it. Prosperity flows forward through me."

Step 4: Close the notebook and place it somewhere sacred to you.

Step 5: Revisit monthly.

Spell 3 – Contract Severing Spell

Materials Needed: Black thread, scissors.

Steps:

Step 1: Hold the thread taut between both hands.

Step 2: Say:

"Unconscious contracts dissolve. I am not bound by inherited limits."

Step 3: Cut the thread cleanly.

Step 4: Bury or discard it intentionally.

Step 5: Take one financial action within 24 hours as proof of release.

Exercises

Exercise 1 – Family Pattern Mapping

Step 1: List major financial events from parents or guardians.
Step 2: Identify repeating themes.
Step 3: Circle patterns you recognize in yourself.
Step 4: Write one boundary you are setting against repetition.
Step 5: Create a measurable financial goal opposing the old pattern.

Exercise 2 – Sovereign Ledger Creation

Step 1: Write current income sources.

Step 2: Write monthly expenses clearly.

Step 3: Calculate surplus or deficit.

Step 4: Assign every dollar a purpose.

Step 5: Set one 90-day measurable target.

Exercise 3 – Emotional Deactivation

Step 1: Identify one money trigger.
Step 2: Sit quietly and breathe deeply for 5 minutes.
Step 3: Write the worst-case scenario fear.
Step 4: Write three rational counterpoints.
Step 5: Take one small corrective action immediately.

Financial Ideas

Legacy Reversal Strategy

If your lineage struggled with saving, prioritize building a visible savings account first—even modest. Visibility disrupts inherited beliefs. Watching growth counters scarcity narratives.

Automate contributions to remove emotional hesitation. Consistency rewires expectation.

Celebrate progress privately or publicly. Positive reinforcement builds new lineage memory.

Income Expansion Through Education

Identify one skill that increases earning potential. Take a focused course or self-study plan. Education shifts trajectory.

Investing in skill-building reframes money from survival to leverage.

Higher-value skills increase negotiating power and opportunity flow.

Structured Generosity Practice

If your lineage feared loss, practice structured generosity—planned giving within budget. This signals abundance without recklessness.

Generosity with structure builds confidence and dissolves hoarding anxiety.

Prosperity grows when giving and receiving feel balanced rather than dangerous.

Meditation – Ash to Architecture

Step 1: Sit comfortably with eyes closed.
Step 2: Inhale slowly for 4 counts, exhale for 6. Repeat 10 times.
Step 3: Visualize a large book labeled "Inherited Ledger."
Step 4: Imagine placing it into a contained fire.
Step 5: Watch it burn calmly, turning into ash.
Step 6: See the ash settle into soil.
Step 7: From the soil, visualize a structure rising—a new financial blueprint.
Step 8: Repeat internally: "I build from clarity."
Step 9: Ask: "What is my next sovereign action?"
Step 10: Open your eyes and write it down.

Journal Prompts

1. What money belief did I inherit that no longer serves me?
2. How have I unconsciously repeated financial patterns?
3. What does sovereignty feel like emotionally?
4. What fears arise when I imagine surpassing my lineage?
5. How can I honor resilience without copying limitation?
6. What is my clearest financial boundary?
7. What does a sovereign ledger look like?
8. How does releasing guilt change my strategy?
9. What would wealth mean for future generations?
10. What action proves the ledger has burned?

Closing Reflection

Burning the ledger is not rebellion. It is responsibility. You are not rejecting your past—you are refining it.

Ancestral patterns end when someone chooses differently. Let that someone be you. Let the fire cleanse shame and leave wisdom. Let ash fertilize structure.

You are not cursed.
You are conscious.
And consciousness is the beginning of wealth.

Chapter Four – Wings of Passive Gain

The Nature of Passive Flight

Passive income is often misunderstood as effortless income. In reality, it is front-loaded discipline that later generates sustained return. Wings are not decorations; they are structures built over time that eventually make flight appear natural.

Energetic imprinting begins with identity. If you believe income only comes from exhaustion, you will unconsciously resist systems that pay you while you sleep. If you believe money must always equal struggle, you will sabotage scalable opportunities.

Passive gain is the art of building once and earning repeatedly. It is intellectual property, automated systems, assets, royalties, dividends, and leveraged skill. It is the decision to detach income from constant physical presence.

Energetically, passive income requires delayed gratification. You plant seeds before harvest. You create before applause. You build before validation.

Wings form quietly before lift becomes visible.

Imprinting the Prosperity Field

Energetic imprinting is the repetition of belief plus behavior until it solidifies into expectation. Expectation shifts posture. Posture shifts action. Action shifts results.

If your internal field expects scarcity, you will underprice, underbuild, and under-leverage. If your field expects scalable wealth, you begin designing differently. You think in systems instead of hours.

Imprinting happens through ritual, repetition, and reinforcement. It happens when you repeatedly affirm your identity as a builder of assets, not merely a seller of time.

Energetically, imprinting requires consistency more than intensity. Small daily reinforcement outperforms sporadic bursts of motivation.

Your nervous system must believe passive gain is safe before it will allow expansion.

From Labor to Leverage

Labor exchanges time for money. Leverage multiplies effort through structure. Wings of passive gain are built from leverage.

Leverage can be digital products, books, courses, licensing, affiliate systems, rentals, subscriptions, dividends, or automated service models. The principle is the same: create once, distribute repeatedly.

Psychologically, leverage requires letting go of constant control. You must allow systems to operate without your moment-to-moment interference.

Energetically, leverage expands field influence. Your impact extends beyond physical presence.

You are not abandoning work. You are restructuring it.

The Myth of Instant Abundance

Passive income does not appear because you desire it. It appears because you structure for it. Many abandon the process too early because initial returns are small.

The imprint must outlast doubt. The builder must trust delayed reward. The moth does not reach the horizon in one flap.

Energetically, impatience collapses expansion. It signals insecurity. Security grows through repetition and patience.

Psychologically, compounding is invisible at first. But invisible growth is still growth.

Wings strengthen gradually.

Designing Wealth Streams

Wealth streams begin as ideas. Ideas become prototypes. Prototypes become assets. Assets become recurring flow.

Start with what you already know. Convert skill into product. Convert experience into guidance. Convert systems into templates.

Energetically, focus on value creation, not extraction. When value is clear, attraction follows naturally.

Passive gain requires clarity, structure, and distribution.

Wings are engineered, not wished into existence.

Sustaining the Flight

Once passive systems begin producing, maintenance replaces hustle. Review, refine, optimize. Remove friction points. Enhance visibility.

Energetically, gratitude stabilizes growth. Acknowledging progress strengthens imprinting.

Psychologically, resist the urge to sabotage success through overcomplication. Keep systems simple.

Flight feels natural only because groundwork was disciplined.

Passive gain is freedom built through architecture.

Financial Tip: Build One Asset at a Time

Choose one passive income idea and commit to finishing it before starting another. Splitting attention weakens imprinting and delays completion.

Allocate specific weekly time blocks dedicated only to asset creation. Consistency compounds.

Once launched, track metrics monthly. Adjust strategically rather than emotionally. Completion builds momentum.

Ritual – The Wing Activation Rite

Materials Needed:
White candle, gold candle, paper, pen, small feather (or symbolic object).

Steps:
Step 1: Write one passive income stream you will build within 90 days.
Step 2: Light the white candle and say: "I clear resistance to scalable wealth."
Step 3: Light the gold candle and say: "I activate systems that earn beyond my hours."
Step 4: Hold the feather and visualize yourself working once and earning repeatedly.
Step 5: Place the feather on the paper and draw two wings around your income idea.
Step 6: Speak: "What I build now continues to provide."
Step 7: Fold the paper toward you and place it somewhere visible.
Step 8: Take one concrete action within 24 hours toward launching the asset.

Spell 1 – Compounding Flame Spell

Materials Needed: Green candle, notebook.

Steps:

Step 1: Light the green candle.

Step 2: Write one scalable idea.

Step 3: Speak:

"Small beginnings, multiplied returns. What I plant now compounds."

Step 4: Visualize steady monthly growth.

Step 5: Extinguish candle and commit to weekly progress sessions.

Spell 2 – Leverage Alignment Spell

Materials Needed: Blue candle, string.

Steps:

Step 1: Light the candle.

Step 2: Stretch string between hands.

Step 3: Say:

"My effort extends beyond this moment. My work echoes into profit."

Step 4: Visualize customers receiving your asset without your presence.

Step 5: Tie the string in a loop and keep as reminder of scalable structure.

Spell 3 – Distribution Path Spell

Materials Needed: White candle, three small objects.

Steps:

Step 1: Light the candle.

Step 2: Place three objects in a line (symbolizing distribution channels).

Step 3: Speak:

"What I create finds its audience."

Step 4: Name three platforms or methods for distribution.

Step 5: Take one step toward setting up one channel within 48 hours.

Exercises

Exercise 1 – Asset Mapping

Step 1: List five skills you possess.
Step 2: Circle one scalable skill.
Step 3: Brainstorm three ways to package it.
Step 4: Choose the simplest version.
Step 5: Outline steps to launch within 30 days.

Exercise 2 – Systemization Audit

Step 1: Identify repetitive tasks in your work.

Step 2: Determine which can be automated.

Step 3: Research one automation tool.

Step 4: Implement a test automation.

Step 5: Measure time saved.

Exercise 3 – Distribution Expansion

Step 1: Identify your current audience source.

Step 2: List two additional platforms.

Step 3: Create one piece of content tailored for each.

Step 4: Publish within one week.

Step 5: Track engagement.

Financial Ideas

Digital Product Creation

Create a digital guide, template, or micro-course based on existing knowledge. Low overhead means higher margin.

Price accessibly to test demand. Gather feedback for refinement.

Once proven, scale through bundles or licensing.

Subscription Model Development

Offer recurring value monthly. Memberships provide predictable income.

Focus on solving one specific problem consistently.

Retention grows through community and reliability.

Royalty-Based Assets

Write, record, or design content that earns repeatedly—books, music, templates.

Distribute widely across platforms to increase reach.

Royalty streams compound over time when nurtured.

Meditation – Winged Expansion Visualization

Step 1: Sit upright and close eyes.
Step 2: Inhale for 4 counts, exhale for 6, repeat 10 times.
Step 3: Visualize small wings forming behind you.
Step 4: See yourself building an asset steadily.
Step 5: Imagine it reaching people while you rest.
Step 6: Watch income flowing in calmly and consistently.
Step 7: Repeat: "I build once and receive repeatedly."
Step 8: Feel gratitude for systems working in background.
Step 9: Ask: "What is my next build step?"
Step 10: Open eyes and write it down.

Journal Prompts

1. What belief prevents me from building passive income?
2. What skill could I scale?
3. Where do I confuse effort with value?
4. What system can I build this quarter?
5. How do I respond to delayed results?
6. What does financial flight feel like?
7. What automation could free time?
8. How does compounding change perspective?
9. What platform aligns with my strengths?
10. Who benefits from my scalable work?

Closing Reflection

Wings of passive gain are built through disciplined creation and reinforced identity. Passive income is not escape from work—it is evolution of work.

Imprint abundance through repetition. Structure before scaling. Build before flight.

The moth once feared flame.
Now it rides thermal currents of its own making.

Chapter Five – Your Flame is the Currency

The Nature of Personal Flame

Every creator carries a flame—an inner current of intensity, obsession, devotion, and lived experience. This flame is not personality alone. It is the energetic charge behind your voice, your ideas, your offers, and your presence.

Most people attempt to sell products. High-magnetism creators transmit fire. Buyers do not respond to information alone—they respond to charge. They feel conviction. They feel clarity. They feel certainty.

Your flame is built from survival, discipline, repetition, and lived transformation. It is refined through pain converted into skill. It is strengthened through consistency and embodied proof.

If you dim your flame to avoid criticism, your offers lose magnetism. If you exaggerate your flame without structure, your offers lose trust. Magnetism requires both intensity and containment.

Your flame is the currency. The offer is merely the container.

Death Moth Charge and Offer Alchemy

The Death Moth represents fearless attraction to illumination. In this chapter, it symbolizes bold visibility—the willingness to let your flame be seen without apology.

Offer alchemy occurs when you infuse skill with conviction. The market is saturated with information but starved for embodied authority. Authority is felt when you have walked the path yourself.

Energetically, Death Moth charge amplifies clarity. You stop hedging. You stop apologizing. You state your offer with precision. Precision increases trust.

Psychologically, magnetism grows when self-doubt decreases. When you believe in your transformation, your posture shifts. Your voice steadies. Your pricing strengthens.

Charge without chaos. Confidence without arrogance. Flame with structure.

Magnetism is Clarity Plus Confidence

Confusion repels. Clarity attracts. If your offer is vague, your field becomes diffuse. If your value is ambiguous, your magnetism weakens.

Clarity answers three questions: Who is this for? What specific problem does it solve? What measurable result does it produce? When these are sharp, attraction strengthens.

Confidence comes from proof. Proof can be lived experience, documented results, client outcomes, or structured methodology. Without proof, flame feels theatrical. With proof, flame feels trustworthy.

Energetically, magnetism increases when alignment exists between identity and offer. If you claim authority but internally doubt it, the charge splits.

Unify identity and delivery. That is the core of high-magnetism creation.

Containment of the Flame

Uncontained fire burns indiscriminately. Contained fire forges metal. The difference is structure.

Your offer must have boundaries. Clear deliverables. Defined timeline. Specific transformation. Containment builds trust.

Energetically, structure grounds intensity. It ensures your passion does not become overwhelm. It ensures your clients feel guided rather than engulfed.

Psychologically, containment strengthens confidence. When you know the limits of your offer, you sell without fear.

Flame plus framework equals currency.

Pricing as Signal

Price communicates positioning. Underpricing signals uncertainty. Overpricing without proof signals ego. Strategic pricing signals value.

When your flame is embodied, pricing becomes a reflection of transformation delivered, not time spent. You are not selling hours. You are selling outcomes.

Energetically, pricing alignment reduces resentment. When compensated fairly, you deliver with greater vitality. When underpaid, your flame dims.

Psychologically, raising prices requires identity expansion. You must believe you are worthy of the exchange.

Currency responds to conviction.

Visibility and Transmission

Your flame cannot attract if hidden. Visibility is transmission. Transmission requires courage.

Fear of criticism often keeps creators invisible. Yet invisibility guarantees stagnation. The Death Moth charge embraces exposure as growth.

Energetically, visibility expands reach. It multiplies opportunities. It increases feedback loops that refine offers.

Psychologically, repetition reduces fear. The more you show up, the less threat visibility holds.

Your flame must be seen to be spent.

Financial Tip: Strengthen One Core Offer

Instead of creating multiple weak offers, refine one high-magnetism offer until it converts consistently. Focus increases energetic charge and simplifies messaging.

Clarify transformation, testimonials, and delivery structure. Remove unnecessary complexity.

Once conversion is stable, expand. Strong foundations amplify flame.

Ritual – The Flame Currency Rite

Materials Needed:

Red candle, gold candle, paper, pen, small mirror.

Steps:

Step 1: Write your core offer at the top of the paper.
Step 2: Under it, write the specific transformation it delivers.
Step 3: Light the red candle and say: "I activate my inner flame."
Step 4: Light the gold candle and say: "I convert charge into currency."
Step 5: Look into the mirror and speak your offer aloud clearly.
Step 6: Visualize clients benefiting from your work.
Step 7: Say: "My flame is structured. My value is clear. My currency flows."
Step 8: Fold the paper toward you and place it under your workspace.
Step 9: Take one visibility action within 24 hours (post, pitch, outreach).
Step 10: Extinguish candles with intention.

Spell 1 – Magnetism Amplifier Spell

Materials Needed: Gold candle, notebook.

Steps:

Step 1: Light the candle.

Step 2: Write three reasons your offer changes lives.

Step 3: Speak:

"Clarity attracts. Confidence converts. My flame draws aligned clients."

Step 4: Visualize inquiries arriving.

Step 5: Commit to one promotional action immediately.

Spell 2 – Authority Anchor Spell

Materials Needed: Black candle, small object.

Steps:

Step 1: Light the candle.

Step 2: Hold the object firmly.

Step 3: Speak:

"I claim authority through experience. I teach what I embody."

Step 4: Recall a personal success related to your offer.

Step 5: Place the object where you prepare offers.

Spell 3 – Pricing Alignment Spell

Materials Needed: Green candle, paper.

Steps:

Step 1: Light the candle.

Step 2: Write your current price.

Step 3: Write your aligned price.

Step 4: Speak:

"My pricing reflects transformation, not fear."

Step 5: Decide on an implementation date and schedule it.

Exercises

Exercise 1 – Offer Clarity Audit

Step 1: Write your offer in one sentence.
Step 2: Define the exact audience.
Step 3: Define the measurable outcome.
Step 4: Remove vague language.
Step 5: Test the sentence on three people for clarity.

Exercise 2 – Proof Compilation

Step 1: List personal results related to your offer.

Step 2: List client or peer feedback.

Step 3: Organize into testimonials or case examples.

Step 4: Add data if available.

Step 5: Integrate into sales messaging.

Exercise 3 – Visibility Challenge

Step 1: Identify one platform.
Step 2: Create three pieces of value-driven content.
Step 3: Publish consistently over one week.
Step 4: Track engagement.
Step 5: Adjust messaging based on response.

Financial Ideas

Signature Program Development

Create one flagship offer with defined structure and transformation. High-ticket offers reduce reliance on volume.

Build strong onboarding and delivery system to ensure consistency.

Refine based on feedback before expanding.

Tiered Offer Strategy

Develop three levels: entry, mid-tier, premium. This allows clients to self-select based on readiness.

Clear differentiation strengthens conversion.

Each tier should maintain aligned transformation promise.

Intellectual Property Licensing

Package your framework for licensing to others. This extends reach beyond personal time.

Create clear usage guidelines.

Licensing transforms expertise into scalable asset.

Meditation – Flame Transmission Alignment

Step 1: Sit upright and close eyes.
Step 2: Breathe in for 4 counts, out for 6, repeat 10 times.
Step 3: Visualize a flame in your chest.
Step 4: See it growing brighter without becoming chaotic.
Step 5: Imagine your offer forming within the flame.
Step 6: See people drawn to its light.
Step 7: Repeat silently: "My value radiates clearly."
Step 8: Feel confidence settling in body.
Step 9: Ask: "What action spreads my flame today?"
Step 10: Open eyes and write it down.

Journal Prompts

1. What makes my offer powerful?
2. Where do I dim my flame?
3. What fear limits visibility?
4. What transformation do I truly deliver?
5. How does pricing reflect self-worth?
6. What proof strengthens my authority?
7. Who is my ideal client?
8. What platform aligns with my voice?
9. How does confidence feel physically?
10. What bold step will I take this week?

Closing Reflection

Your flame is not ego. It is earned intensity refined into service. When structured properly, it becomes currency.

Magnetism grows from clarity, confidence, and containment. Visibility spreads transmission. Pricing signals authority.

The Death Moth charge is not reckless attraction—it is disciplined luminosity.

Let your flame be seen.
Let it be structured.
Let it be exchanged.

Appendix A – 11 Flame-Initiated Wealth Invocations

These invocations are not passive affirmations. They are activation statements. Each one is designed to be spoken aloud with breath, posture, and intention. Read them slowly. Stand or sit upright. Let your voice carry conviction. Wealth responds to clarity and embodiment.

Invocation I – The Ignition of Sovereignty

I stand in financial sovereignty.
I release inherited scarcity and claim conscious creation.
My income is not an accident—it is architecture.
My decisions are not reactions—they are direction.
What I build reflects who I am becoming.
I no longer shrink to survive.
I expand with structure.
I earn with integrity.
I multiply with discipline.
My flame answers to no fear.

Invocation II – The Discipline of Compounding

What I repeat, strengthens.
What I automate, stabilizes.
What I track, improves.
My discipline compounds daily.
Small actions become large results.
Consistency outperforms intensity.
I build assets patiently.
I honor delayed gratification.
I value structure over impulse.
My steady flame becomes unstoppable growth.

Invocation III – The Conversion of Debt

Debt does not define me.
Debt is compressed experience awaiting direction.
I convert obligation into opportunity.
I meet numbers without shame.
I apply strategy without hesitation.
I bind my focus to repayment and expansion.
I dissolve avoidance.
I multiply momentum.
I honor responsibility.
My flame transforms weight into fuel.

Invocation IV – The Authority of Pricing

My value is clear.
My pricing reflects transformation, not fear.
I do not undercharge to be liked.
I do not overcharge without structure.
I stand firmly in fair exchange.
Currency flows toward confidence.
Clarity attracts alignment.
Authority invites respect.
My offer delivers measurable change.
My flame is worth the exchange.

Invocation V – The Magnetism of Visibility

I allow myself to be seen.
I speak with precision.
I transmit with conviction.
My voice carries experience.
My presence carries proof.
I do not hide brilliance to protect comfort.
I welcome aligned attention.
I filter misalignment without collapse.
I show up consistently.
My flame attracts what is meant for me.

Invocation VI – The Architecture of Passive Gain

I build once and receive repeatedly.
I design systems that outlast my hours.
I leverage knowledge into assets.
I structure income beyond exhaustion.
My ideas become recurring value.
My efforts echo into profit.
I commit to completion.
I refine before expanding.
Compounding is my ally.
My flame powers sustainable freedom.

Invocation VII – The Release of Ancestral Limitation

What was inherited unconsciously is now examined.
What was repeated without choice is now ended.
I honor resilience without copying restriction.
I release financial guilt.
I release scarcity loyalty.
I step beyond lineage limitation.
I redefine prosperity forward.
My growth does not betray my roots.
It elevates them.
My flame carries a new standard.

Invocation VIII – The Expansion of Skill

My skills are valuable.
My experience holds currency.
I refine my craft continually.
I increase my earning capacity intentionally.
Education expands opportunity.
Practice strengthens confidence.
I monetize ethically.
I build offers that solve real problems.
I align talent with demand.
My flame grows brighter through mastery.

Invocation IX – The Stabilization of Wealth

Income enters calmly.
Expenses are managed clearly.
Savings grow consistently.
Investments are chosen wisely.
I assign every dollar a purpose.
Structure protects expansion.
Planning replaces panic.
Review replaces avoidance.
Order replaces chaos.
My flame burns steady, not erratic.

Invocation X – The Courage of Expansion

I expand beyond old limits.
I stretch without breaking.
Growth feels safe in my body.
Risk is measured, not reckless.
I trust structured leaps.
I learn from feedback.
I refine through data.
I adapt without collapse.
I move forward without apology.
My flame rises with confidence.

Invocation XI – The Embodiment of Wealth Identity

I am a builder of assets.
I am a steward of resources.
I am disciplined and decisive.
I think in systems, not scarcity.
I operate from sovereignty.
My mindset aligns with multiplication.
My actions align with architecture.
My habits align with prosperity.
My identity aligns with abundance.
My flame is the currency I circulate.

Closing Reflection

Invocations are not magic words; they are mirrors. When spoken consistently, they reshape internal posture. When paired with disciplined action, they accelerate transformation.

Your flame is strengthened by repetition. Your wealth is stabilized by structure. Speak these invocations daily—not mechanically, but intentionally. Stand when you say them. Breathe deeply. Feel them settle into your nervous system.

Wealth is not summoned by wishful thinking. It is anchored by identity, reinforced by discipline, and expanded by courageous visibility.

Return to these invocations whenever doubt rises.
Return to them when momentum builds.
Return to them when you forget your strength.

Your flame is active.
Your structure is forming.
Your prosperity is not accidental—it is embodied.

Message from the Author:

I hope you enjoyed this book, I love astrology and knew there was not a book such as this out on the shelf. I love metaphysical items as well. Please check out my other books:

-Life of Government Benefits

-My life of Hell

-My life with Hydrocephalus

-Red Sky

-World Domination:Woman's rule

-World Domination:Woman's Rule 2: The War

-Life and Banishment of Apophis: book 1

-The Kidney Friendly Diet

-The Ultimate Hemp Cookbook

-Creating a Dispensary(legally)

-Cleanliness throughout life: the importance of showering from childhood to adulthood.

-Strong Roots: The Risks of Overcoddling children

-Hemp Horoscopes: Cosmic Insights and Earthly Healing

- Celestial Hemp Navigating the Zodiac: Through the Green Cosmos

-Astrological Hemp: Aligning The Stars with Earth's Ancient Herb

-The Astrological Guide to Hemp: Stars, Signs, and Sacred Leaves

-Green Growth: Innovative Marketing Strategies for your Hemp Products and Dispensary

-Cosmic Cannabis

-Astrological Munchies

-Henry The Hemp

-Zodiacal Roots: The Astrological Soul Of Hemp

- **Green Constellations: Intersection of Hemp and Zodiac**

-Hemp in The Houses: An astrological Adventure Through The Cannabis Galaxy

-Galactic Ganja Guide

Heavenly Hemp

Zodiac Leaves
Doctor Who Astrology
Cannastrology
Stellar Satvias and Cosmic Indicas
Celestial Cannabis: A Zodiac Journey
AstroHerbology: The Sky and The Soil: Volume 1
AstroHerbology:Celestial Cannabis:Volume 2
Cosmic Cannabis Cultivation
The Starry Guide to Herbal Harmony: Volume 1
The Starry Guide to Herbal Harmony: Cannabis Universe: Volume 2
Yugioh Astrology: Astrological Guide to Deck, Duels and more
Nightmare Mansion: Echoes of The Abyss
Nightmare Mansion 2: Legacy of Shadows
Nightmare Mansion 3: Shadows of the Forgotten
Nightmare Mansion 4: Echoes of the Damned
The Life and Banishment of Apophis: Book 2
Nightmare Mansion: Halls of Despair
Healing with Herb: Cannabis and Hydrocephalus
Planetary Pot: Aligning with Astrological Herbs: Volume 1
Fast Track to Freedom: 30 Days to Financial Independence Using AI, Assets, and Agile Hustles
Cosmic Hemp Pathways
How to Become Financially Free in 30 Days: 10,000 Paths to Prosperity
Zodiacal Herbage: Astrological Insights: Volume 1
Nightmare Mansion: Whispers in the Walls
The Daleks Invade Atlantis
Henry the hemp and Hydrocephalus

10X The Kidney Friendly Diet
Cannabis Universe: Adult coloring book
Hemp Astrology: The Healing Power of the Stars

Zodiacal Herbage: Astrological Insights: Cannabis Universe: Volume 2

Planetary Pot: Aligning with Astrological Herbs: Cannabis Universes: Volume 2

Doctor Who: Convergence Protocol – The Replicator War

Nightmare Mansion: Curse of the Blood Moon

The Celestial Stoner: A Guide to the Zodiac

Cosmic Pleasures: Sex Toy Astrology for Every Sign

Hydrocephalus Astrology: Navigating the Stars and Healing Waters

Lapis and the Mischievous Chocolate Bar

Celestial Positions: Sexual Astrology for Every Sign

Apophis's Shadow Work Journal: **:** A Journey of Self-Discovery and Healing

Kinky Cosmos: Sexual Kink Astrology for Every Sign

Digital Cosmos: The Astrological Digimon Compendium

Stellar Seeds: The Cosmic Guide to Growing with Astrology

Apophis's Daily Gratitude Journal

Cat Astrology: Feline Mysteries of the Cosmos

The Cosmic Kama Sutra: An Astrological Guide to Sexual Positions

Unleash Your Potential: A Guided Journal Powered by AI Insights

Whispers of the Enchanted Grove

Cosmic Pleasures: An Astrological Guide to Sexual Kinks

369, 12 Manifestation Journal

Whisper of the nocturne journal(blank journal for writing or drawing)

The Boogey Book

Locked In Reflection: A Chastity Journey Through Locktober

Generating Wealth Quickly:How to Generate $100,000 in 24 Hours

Star Magic: Harness the Power of the Universe

The Flatulence Chronicles: A Fart Journal for Self-Discovery

The Doctor and The Death Moth

Seize the Day: A Personal Seizure Tracking Journal

The Ultimate Boogeyman Safari: A Journey into the Boogie World and Beyond

Whispers of Samhain: 1,000 Spells of Love, Luck, and Lunar Magic: Samhain Spell Book

Apophis's guides:Witch's Spellbook Crafting Guide for Halloween

Frost & Flame: The Enchanted Yule Grimoire of 1000 Winter Spells

The Ultimate Boogey Goo Guide & Spooky Activities for Halloween Fun

Harmony of the Scales: A Libra's Spellcraft for Balance and Beauty

The Enchanted Advent: 36 Days of Christmas Wonders

Nightmare Mansion: The Labyrinth of Screams

Harvest of Enchantment: 1,000 Spells of Gratitude, Love, and Fortune for Thanksgiving

The Boogey Chronicles: A Journal of Nightly Encounters and Shadowy Secrets

The 12 Days of Financial Freedom: A Step-by-Step Christmas Countdown to Transform Your Finances

Sigil of the Eternal Spiral Blank Journal

A Christmas Feast: Timeless Recipes for Every Meal

Holiday Stress-Free Solutions: A Survival Guide to Thriving During the Festive Season

Yu-Gi-Oh! Holiday Gifting Mastery: The Ultimate Guide for Fans and Newcomers Alike

Holiday Harmony: A Hydrocephalus Survival Guide for the Festive Season

Celestial Craft: The Witch's Almanac for 2025 – A Cosmic Guide to Manifestations, Moons, and Mystical Events

Doctor Who: The Toymaker's Winter Wonderland

Tulsa King Unveiled: A Thrilling Guide to Stallone's Mafia Masterpiece

Pendulum Craft: A Complete Guide to Crafting and Using Personalized Divination Tools

Nightmare Mansion: Santa's Eternal Eve

Starlight Noel: A Cosmic Journey through Christmas Mysteries

The Dark Architect: Unlocking the Blueprint of Existence

Surviving the Embrace: The Ultimate Guide to Encounters with The Hugging Molly

The Enchanted Codex: Secrets of the Craft for Witches, Wiccans, and Pagans

Harvest of Gratitude: A Complete Thanksgiving Guide

Yuletide Essentials: A Complete Guide to an Authentic and Magical Christmas

Celestial Smokes: A Cosmic Guide to Cigars and Astrology

Living in Balance: A Comprehensive Survival Guide to Thriving with Diabetes Insipidus

Cosmic Symbiosis: The Venom Zodiac Chronicles

The Cursed Paw of Ambition

Cosmic Symbiosis: The Astrological Venom Journal

Celestial Wonders Unfold: A Stargazer's Guide to the Cosmos (2024-2029)

The Ultimate Black Friday Prepper's Guide: Mastering Shopping Strategies and Savings

Cosmic Sales: The Astrological Guide to Black Friday Shopping

Legends of the Corn Mother and Other Harvest Myths

Whispers of the Harvest: The Corn Mother's Journal

The Evergreen Spellbook

The Doctor Meets the Boogeyman

The White Witch of Rose Hall's SpellBook

The Gingerbread Golem's Shadow: A Study in Sweet Darkness

The Gingerbread Golem Codex: An Academic Exploration of Sweet Myths

The Gingerbread Golem Grimoire: Sweet Magicks and Spells for the Festive Witch

The Curse of the Gingerbread Golem

10-minute Christmas Crafts for kids

Christmas Crisis Solutions: The Ultimate Last-Minute Survival Guide

Gingerbread Golem Recipes: Holiday Treats with a Magical Twist

The Infinite Key: Unlocking Mystical Secrets of the Ages

Enchanted Yule: A Wiccan and Pagan Guide to a Magical and Memorable Season

Dinosaurs of Power: Unlocking Ancient Magick

Astro-Dinos: The Cosmic Guide to Prehistoric Wisdom

Gallifrey's Yule Logs: A Festive Doctor Who Cookbook

The Dino Grimoire: Secrets of Prehistoric Magick

The Gift They Never Knew They Needed

The Gingerbread Golem's Culinary Alchemy: Enchanting Recipes for a Sweetly Dark Feast

A Time Lord Christmas: Holiday Adventures with the Doctor

Krampusproofing Your Home: Defensive Strategies for Yule

Silent Frights: A Collection of Christmas Creepypastas to Chill Your Bones

Santa Raptor's Jolly Carnage: A Dino-Claus Christmas Tale

Prehistoric Palettes: A Dino Wicca Coloring Journey

The Christmas Wishkeeper Chronicles

The Starlight Sleigh: A Holiday Journey

Elf Secrets: The True Magic of the North Pole

Candy Cane Conjurations

Cooking with Kids: Recipes Under 20 Minutes

Doctor Who: The TARDIS Confiscation

The Anxiety First Aid Kit: Quick Tools to Calm Your Mind

Frosty Whispers: A Winter's Tale

The Infinite Key: Unlocking the Secrets to Prosperity, Resilience, and Purpose

The Grasping Void: Why You'll Regret This Purchase

Astrology for Busy Bees: Star Signs Simplified

The Instant Focus Formula: Cut Through the Noise

The Secret Language of Colors: Unlocking the Emotional Codes

Sacred Fossil Chronicles: Blank Journal

The Christmas Cottage Miracle

Feeding Frenzy: Graboid-Inspired Recipes

Manifest in Minutes: The Quick Law of Attraction Guide

The Symbiote Chronicles: Doctor Who's Venomous Journey

Think Tiny, Grow Big: The Minimalist Mindset

The Energy Key: Unlocking Limitless Motivation

New Year, New Magic: Manifesting Your Best Year Yet

Unstoppable You: Mastering Confidence in Minutes

Infinite Energy: The Secret to Never Feeling Drained

Lightning Focus: Mastering the Art of Productivity in a Distracted World

Saturnalia Manifestation Magick: A Guide to Unlocking Abundance During the Solstice

Graboids and Garland: The Ultimate Tremors-Themed Christmas Guide

12 Nights of Holiday Magic

The Power of Pause: 60-Second Mindfulness Practices

The Quick Reset: How to Reclaim Your Life After Burnout

The Shadow Eater: A Tale of Despair and Survival

The Micro-Mastery Method: Transform Your Skills in Just Minutes a Day

Reclaiming Time: How to Live More by Doing Less

Chronovore: The Eternal Nexus

The Mind Reset: Unlocking Your Inner Peace in a Chaotic World

Confidence Code: Building Unshakable Self-Belief

Baby the Vampire Terrier
Baby the Vampire Terrier's Christmas Adventure
Celestial Streams: The Content Creator's Astrology Manual
The Wealth Whisperer: Unlocking Abundance with Everyday Actions
The Energy Equation: Maximize Your Output Without Burning Out
The Happiness Algorithm: Science-Backed Steps to Joyful Living
Stress-Free Success: Achieving Goals Without Anxiety
Mindful Wealth: The New Blueprint for Financial Freedom
The Festive Flavors of New Year: A Culinary Celebration
The Master's Gambit: Keys of Eternal Power
Shadowed Secrets: Groundhog Day Mysteries
Beneath the Burrow: Lessons from the Groundhog
Spring's Whispers: The Groundhog's Prediction
The Limitless Mindset: Unlock Your Untapped Potential
The Focus Funnel: How to Cut Through Chaos and Get Results
Bold Moves: Building Courage to Live on Your Terms
The Daily Shift: Simple Practices for Lasting Transformation
The Quarter-Life Reset: Thriving in Your 20s and 30s
The Art of Shadowplay: Building Your Own Personal Myth
The Eternal Loop: Finding Purpose in Repetition
Burrowing Wisdom: Life Lessons from the Groundhog
Shadow Work: A Groundhog Day Perspective
Love in Bloom: 5-Minute Romantic Gestures
The Shadowspell Codex: Secrets of Forbidden Magick
The Burnout Cure: Finding Balance in a Busy World
The Groundhog Prophecy: Unlocking Seasonal Secrets
Nog Tales: The Spirited History of Eggnog
Six More Weeks: Embracing Seasonal Transitions
The Lumivian Chronicles: Fragments of the Fifth Dimension
Money on Your Mind: A Beginner's Guide to Wealth
The Focus Fix: Breaking Through Distraction

January's Spirit Keepers: Mystical Protectors of the Cold
Creativity Unchained: Unlocking Your Wildest Ideas in 2025
Manifestation Mastery: 365 Days to Rewrite Your Reality
The Groundhog's Mirror: Reflecting on Change
The Weeping Angels' Christmas Curse
Burrowed in Time: A Groundhog Day Journey
Heartbeats: Poems to Share with Your Valentine
Dino Wicca: The Sacred Grimoire of Prehistoric Magick
Courage of the Pride: Finding Your Inner Roar
The Lion's Leap: Bold Moves for Big Results
Healthy Hustle: Achieving Without Overworking
Practical Manifesting: Turning Dreams into Reality in 2025
Jurassic Pharaohs: Unlocking the Magick of Ancient Egypt and Dino Wicca
The Happiness Equation: Small Changes for Big Joy
The Confidence Compass: Finding Your Inner Strength
Whispers in the Hollow: Tales of the Forgotten Beasts
Echoes from the Hollow: The Return of Forgotten Beasts
The Hollow Ascendant: The Rise of the Forgotten Beasts
The Relationship Reset: Building Better Connections
Mastering the Morning: How to Win the Day Before 8 AM
The Shadow's Dance: Groundhog Day Symbolism
Cupid's Kitchen: Quick Valentine's Day Recipes
Valentine's Day on a Budget: Love Without Breaking the Bank
Astrocraft: Aligning the Stars in the World of Minecraft
Forecasting Life: Groundhog Day Reflections
Bleeding Hearts: Twisted Tales of Valentine's Terror
Herbal Smoke Revolution: The Ultimate Guide to Nature's Cigarette Alternative
Winter's Wrath: The Complete Survival Blueprint for Extreme Freezes.
The Groundhog's Shadow: A Tale of Seasons
Burrowed Insights: Wisdom from the Groundhog

Sensual Strings: The Art of Erotic Bondage
Whispered Flames: Unlocking the Power of Fire Play
Forgotten Shadows: A Guide to Cryptids Lost to Time
Six Weeks of Secrets: Groundhog Day's Hidden Messages
Shadows and Cycles: Groundhog Day Reflections
The Art of Love Letters: Crafting the Perfect Message
Romantic Getaways at Home: Turning Your Space into Paradise
Purrfect Brews: A Cat Lover's Guide to Coffee and Companionship
The Groundhog's Wisdom: Timeless Lessons for Modern Life
The Shadow Oracle: Groundhog Day as a Predictor
Emerging from the Burrow: A Journey of Renewal
The Language of Love: Learning Your Partner's Love Style
Authorpreneur: The Ultimate Blueprint for Writing, Publishing, and Thriving as an Author
Weathering the Seasons: Groundhog Day Perspectives
Valentine's Day Magic: A Guide to Romantic Rituals
The Shadow Chronicles: Stories of Groundhog Day
Love and Laughter: Fun Games for Valentine's Day
AstroRealty: Unlocking the Stars for Property Success
The Groundhog's Path: A Guide to Seasonal Balance
Groundhog Day Diaries: Reflections in the Shadow
The Groundhog's Light: Illuminating the Path Ahead
Valentine's Traditions from Around the World
AI Wealth Revolution: Unlocking the Trillionaire Mindset
Love Rekindled: Reigniting Passion in Relationships
Single and Thriving: Self-Love on Valentine's Day
Emerald Legends: Mystical Tales of Ireland
Green Alchemy: Harnessing Nature's Magic
The Hearts of Horror: A Valentine's Day Nightmare
The Leprechaun's Guide to Wealth and Wisdom
Dancing with the Sidhe: Celebrating the Otherworld

Shamrocks and Shadows: Mysteries of the Green Isle

Emerald Energy: Harnessing Luck and Growth

The Gingerbread Golem's Valentine: A Sweetheart's Guide to Love and Enchantment

The Celtic Knot: Weaving Life and Destiny

Green Fire: Elemental Magic for St. Patrick's Day

Clover Chronicles: Finding Your Inner Luck

Ireland's Mystical Creatures: A Field Guide

Gingerbread Golem's Love Almanac

Prowl and Thrive: The Lion's Guide to Success

Love Alchemy: Transforming Your Life Through Heart Energy

WORLD DOMINATION: Woman's Rule 3:The New Life

The Midnight Rose: A Guide to Lunar Love Spells

The Forbidden Letters: Writing Your Own Love Prophecy

Luck and Lore: St. Patrick's Day for Modern Mystics

The Green Path: A Pagan Celebration of Renewal

The Dark Architect's Guide to Reprogramming Reality

Prankster's Paradise: A Guide to Harmless Hijinks

Manifest Your Reality: The Law of Attraction Simplified

The TARDIS Owner's Manual: Understanding the Doctor's Ship: *A complete guide to the TARDIS, its technology, secrets, and mysteries*

Starlit Romance: Astrology Secrets for Finding True Love

The Time Lord's Atlas: A Complete Guide to the Whoniverse: ***A breakdown of the locations, planets, and dimensions explored in Doctor Who***

Sweetheart Shadows: The Dark Side of Love and Attraction

February Fire: Reigniting Passion in Every Area of Life

The Self-Love Toolkit: 5 Ways to Embrace Who You Are

February Sparks: Ignite Your Dreams in 28 Days

March to Success: A 31-Day Action Blueprint

Ancient Paths: The 13 Sacred Principles of Dino Wicca

Echoes of Tomorrow: Navigating the AI Revolution
The Wellness Blueprint: Balancing Mind, Body, and Soul
Green Horizons: Sustainable Living for a Better Tomorrow
The AI Wealth Code: How to Make Millions with Automation
AI-Powered Creativity: Writing, Art, and Music for Profit
Extinction Rites: Rebirthing Your Soul Through Prehistoric Magick
Sacred Serpents tarot
Celestial Enchantment blank journal
Star Strains
Culinary Journeys: Exploring Global Flavors at Home
The Hollowvale Curse
The Hollowvale Harvest
The Egg of Transformation: Awakening Your Inner Power
Blooming Into Power: A Wiccan Guide to Spring Awakening
The Nightmare Nexus: The Third Doctor's Perilous Haunting
Digital Detox: Reclaiming Your Life in a Connected World
Ostara's Path: Walking the Spiral of Renewal
The Sacred Hare
Financial Freedom: Building Wealth in the Modern Age
Spring's Cauldron: Stirring the Waters of Change
The Hollowvale Pact
Quantum Consciousness: The Science of Reality Shifting
The Hollowvale Hunger
The Sacred Waters Within: A Witch's Guide to Hydrocephalus Magick
The Raven's Nest: Building a Life of Unshakable Stability
AI and the Human Mind: The Future of Intelligence
The Hollowvale Reckoning
Timeless Love: Building and Maintaining Lasting Relationships
The Raven's Roar: Unlocking Unstoppable Confidence
Raven Sight: Awakening Intuition and Inner Wisdom

The Butterfly Effect: Small Changes, Big Transformations
Taming the Boogeyman: How to Conquer Your Inner Fears
The Magick of Green: Awakening Earth's Energy in You
The Entrepreneurial Mindset: Secrets to Business Success
The Hollowvale End
The Shadow Luck Ritual: Reclaiming Power from Your Dark Side
Spring Magick for Beginners: A Simple Guide to Seasonal Energy Work
Doctor Who: The Hollowvale Conundrum
The March of Miracles: Unlocking Synchronicities in Spring
Unveiling the Cosmos: A Guide to Stargazing and Space Exploration
The Ultimate Guide to Surviving an Economic Collapse
The AI Gold Rush: How to Profit from the AI Revolution
Bastet's Shadow: The Hidden Power of Feline Magick
The Bastet Codex: Unlocking the Goddess's Magickal Secrets
Purring Spells: Harnessing Bastet's Healing Frequencies
Bastet's Nine Lives: Rebirth, Transformation, and Immortality Spells
Primal Currents: Hydrocephalus Magick in the Path of Dino Wicca
The Digital Gold Rush: Mastering E-Commerce and Online Sales
Future Shock: Adapting to the Next Decade of Change
The Quantum Mindset: Think Like a Billionaire
Sacred Motherhood: Awakening the Divine Feminine Within
The Mother's Spellbook: Enchantments for Love, Protection, and Prosperity
The Witch's Guide to Parenting: Raising Empowered and Intuitive Children
The Magick of Motherhood: Reclaiming Your Power Through Rituals

The Pagan Path to Self-Love: A Goddess's Guide to Worth and Confidence
Wild Woman Magick: Unleashing Your Primal Power
The Money Magnet Blueprint: Unlocking Unlimited Wealth
Biohacking 101: Unlock Your Body's Full Potential
The Wild Father: A Pagan Guide to Strength and Wisdom
The Sacred Masculine: Unlocking Your Inner Power
The Druid's Compass
The Warrior's Mindset
The Father's Fire
Odin's Path
Ancestral Bonds
The House That Whispers
The Magician's Code
The Wild Hunt
The Green Man's Path
The Altar of Success
The Shadow and the Sword
The High Priestess's Guide to Energy Healing
The Lunar Mother
The Sacred Self-Care Grimoire
The Womb Wisdom Codex
The Wheel of the Mother
The Witch's Guide to Manifestation
The Q2 Reset
The Ultimate Guide to AI-Powered Passive Income
Escape the 9-5
AI Feline Fortunes
The Tear-Stained Grimoire
Razorblade Runes
Cemetery Sirens
The Midnight Wristwatch
The Town That Forgets

AI Horror & Creepypasta
The Hollow Frequency
The Breach Echo
The Quiet Between Worlds
The Sigil of Tharan-Khul
Summon the Vault of Y'ha'ten
The Becoming Codex
The Profit of Az'ra-nar
The Drowned Logos
Echoes of the Eldritch Will
The Deep Ledger
Necronomicon of Networth
Covenant of the Wealthwyrm
The Whisperer's Manifesto
The Rites of Azh-K'luth
The Ark of the Crawling Coin
The Tithe of Shadows
Inkheart Abyss
The Timewinds of Y'ha-nthlei
The Spiral Labyrinth of Azag-Nirrh
The Gallifreyan Heresy of the Black Pharaoh
The Psalms of Nyog-Sotha
Black Rain Alchemy
The Infinite Maw
The Entropic Blueprint
The Oracle of Sh'guul
The Book of Breach
The Drowned Saint's Testament
Dreamcraft of the Sleeper God
The Silence Market
Cthonomics: The Dark Wealth Algorithm
Invocation of the Ten-Eyed King
Wealthbound to the Wyrm Below

Become the Unnameable
Codex of the Sovereign Flame
Rituals of Relentless Becoming
The Shadow Ascends
The Eyes Beneath You
The Will That Wakes Worlds
Silence Is a Weapon
The Mirror That Screams
The Whisper Between Moments
The Mind That Devours Fear
The Myth of the Finished Self
The Architect of Your Madness
The Voice You've Buried
The Discipline of Madness
Stormborn: Awakening Your Inner Tempest
The Mind That Ate Time
Unbind Your Becoming
The Pact You Owe Yourself
The Devourer's Diet
The Acid That Carves the Path
The Tower You Must Burn
The Breath Between Worlds
Speak Like the Deep
The Labyrinth Within
The Spine of the Sea God
Rejection Is a Portal
The Crown You Refused
The Scar Is the Spell
The Lightless Flame
The Habit of Becoming Horrific
ChickenJockey Chaos
The Gatekeeper Within
You Are Not Your Name

The Compass of the Mad
The Archive of Unsent Letters
What the Mirror Can't Show You
The Knife You Needed
Worship Nothing, Become Everything
The Other Voice
The Body the World Forgot
The Vein of the Void
The Black Bone Codex
The Puzzle of the Hidden Self (Millennium Puzzle)
The Eye That Sees the Lie *(Millennium Eye)*
The Ring of Return (Millennium Ring)
The Rod of Relentless Will ***(Millennium Rod)***
The Tally of the Soul (Millennium Tauk/Necklace)
The Key to the Locked Timeline (Millennium Key)
The Scale of Sacred Decisions (Millennium Scales)
Inferno Bites: The UnOfficial Minecraft Lava Cookbook
Rot in the Attic
Prana: The Hidden Force of Your Infinite Self
The Shadow Realm Within: Transforming Darkness Into Destiny
The Borderland Collapse
Claws of Protection: Bastet's Defensive Magick
Mr. Ring-a-Ding's Madness
Yugioh Astrology: Celestial Deckcraft and Duel Destiny (2026–2027 Edition)
The Seal You Signed: Unlocking the Power You Once Feared
The Puzzle of Infinite Minds: Unlocking the Mentalism Hidden Within
The Eye That Mirrors the All: Secrets of Inner Reflection
Doctor Who: The Toymaker's Broadcast
The Rod of Eternal Flow: Commanding the Currents of Vibration

Golden Eyes of Bastet: Enhancing Psychic Vision
The Key of Dual Forces: Balance Within the Polarity
The Scales of Living Rhythm: Timing the Dance of Life
The Necklace of Hidden Cause: Weaving the Webs of Fate
The Ring of Secret Masters: Rising Through the All Within All
Daggers of the Dying Deep
Bastet's Wealth and Fortune Magick: Prosperity Rituals of the Goddess
The Tide that Speaks
The Scrolls of Petosiris: 13 Rituals from the Feathered Eye
Petosiris and the Living Plague of Osirion
Feline Fire: Bastet's Passion and Love Magick
The Star Altar of Petosiris
Bastet's Whiskers: Supernatural Sensory Magick
The Bastet Grimoire
Feeding the Shadows
The Mouthless Prayer
The Spiral Wound
Becoming the Ibis: Lessons from Petosiris's Mind
The Crimson Coven: Cola Magick for Sweet Dominion
Sacred Cat's Paw
The Soda Zodiac: A Flavor for Every Sign
Covenant of the Crawling Flame
The Ink of Ish'Zur
Frothroot: The Thirst That Ate the World
The Golden Glyphs of Prosperity
The Etherbind Codex
Echoes of the Resistance: Reclaiming the You That Survived
Harnessed Minds: Breaking Free from Mental Control
The Eyes in the Smoke
Rootwake: The Carbon Covenant
Skitter Logic: Unlearning the Fear That Built You

Doctor Who: The World That Froths
Rootwake: The Fizz That Rewrites Flesh
Rootwake: Frothfather of the World
The Holly Pact: Blood Beneath the Mistletoe
The 2nd Mass Principle: Building Unbreakable Tribes
Web of Wits: A Survival Guide to Encounters with Anasi the Spider (Aunt Nancy)
The Hexbreaking Handbook: Effective Spells to Remove Curses
Pop Alchemy: Transform Your Life One Sip at a Time
The Mason Code: Leading in Unleadable Times
Petosiris and the Fifth Chamber of Thoth
The Ether Seed Within
The Parent of Tomorrow
Petosiris's Pyramid of Perpetual Wealth
Unlearn the World
Grimoire of the Hollow Tongue
Zodiac Weeds: Finding Your Strain Through the Stars
Aquarius Rises in the Bank
The Sugar God's Smile
The Skinclock Reversal: Biohacking the Face of Time
Debtburn: How to Obliterate What You Owe Forever
The Ice Cream Oracle: What Your Cone Says About Your Future
Silence Is Sovereignty: The Power of Being Unreadable
The Wind That Whispers Through Stone
Path of the Four Directions
Doctor Who: The Maestro's Symphony of Endings
Oxygen Grail: Breathing to Undo the Clock
Zodiacal Collapse: When Stars Devour Time
Teachings from the Red Sand Silence
Doctor Who: Omega – The Broken Equation
Memory Wipe Your Past: Start Over Like a MiB

Mitochondria Prime: Ignite the Core of Youth
A Nest of Roaches
Grub from the Galaxy: MiB Recipes You'll Never Forget
Whiskers of Power: Bastet's Guide to Inner Sovereignty
The Gift Must Cost Them: Negotiation Through Unequal Exchange
The Worm Guys' Wealth Code: Hustle Like an Alien
Bug Out: The Edgar Method for Ruthless Goal Setting
Weaving Life with Spiderwoman's Pattern
Doctor Who: The Rani's Renaissance
How to Get a Job (If You're a Puppygirl)
Speak Through Others: The Art of Proxy Power
T-Rex Your Trauma: Reclaim the Power of Your Primal Self
The Black Briefcase: How MiB Stay Wealthy in Silence
The Thirst Beyond Reason: Understanding Diabetes Insipidus From the Inside Out
Backwoods Witchcraft for Billionaires: The Pagan Path from Dirt Roads to Gold Roads
The Moonshine Grimoire: Fermented Spells for Abundance
The Nameless Geometry
The Wraith's Mixtape: Spellcasting with Songs of Sorrow
The Gallifreyan Gentleman: Silent Wealth, Sonic Confidence, and the Doctor's Code of Living
Sugar Water Confidence
Dino Totems: Spirit Guides from Earth's First Gods
Pumpkin Sigils & Ritual Smoke
The Hózhó Compass
The Distortus Discipline – Order from Inner Mutation
Witchcraft for the Cold-Blooded Soul
Moonlight Over the Blessingway
Water, Interrupted: When the Body Forgets How to Hold On
Deformed but Divine: Embracing Your Asymmetry
Hexes in the Henhouse: The Farm Witch's Guide to Power

The Reversed Flame: A Grimoire of Inverted Power

Salt, Cells, and Sanity: Reclaiming Balance with Diabetes Insipidus

King of the Broken: Crowning the Flawed Self

Moonlight Scars: Emo Moon Magick and the Art of Lunar Sorrow

Noose Spells: Magick of the Hanging Rope

The Goth Cathedral: Rituals of the Broken and Beautiful

The Cretaceous Codex: Dino Spirits and Fossil Magick

The Turkey Bones Ritual

Nine Lives of Manifestation: Unlocking Bastet's Reality Codes

Chaos Muscles: Building Strength from Twisted Pain

Emo Blood Magick: The Veins of Power

The 3AM Flood: Nighttime Urination, Sleep Loss, and the DI Spiral

The Silence Between the Stars

The Lemon Method: Sour Your Way to Success

Starlit Sovereign

The Rite of Twelve Gates: Walking the Gates of the Duat.

Cornbread and Conjure: Recipes for Riches and Rootwork

The Black Rose Rituals: Emo Love Spells and Obsession Magick

The Eternal Goodbye: Death Magick and Rebirth Rituals

Sinkrot: The Drain That Remembers

The Hybrid Mindset: Thinking Beyond Evolution

Bone Dry: Navigating Dehydration Before It Breaks You

Wreathcraft: Winter Sigils and Yuletide Spells

The Rite of Twelve Mouths

S'mores of the Damned: Haunted Recipes for Halloween Night

Rethink the Drink: A Beverage Survival Guide for DI Warriors

The Shadow Chord: Guitar Magick and Sonic

Malformed Yet Majestic: Leading When You Feel Wrong Inside

The Cursed Diary: Ink-Stained Spells of the Emo Soul

Anxiety Off Switch: Emergency Reset for a Fried Nervous System

The Energy Heist: How to Take Back Your Life from Drainers

Beyond the Bathroom: Rebuilding Your Social Life With DI

Coyote's Gift for Decision Makers

Ghoul-Goo: Spooky S'mores You'll Die For

Echoes in the Mirror: Scrying and Self-Destruction Magick

Thread and Thorn: Stitching Spells from Rural Cloth

The Mogwai Mind: Building Untouchable Wealth from Small Ideas

Be Your Own Guide: Trust Your Inner Compass

Hormones in Chaos: The Endocrine Puzzle of Diabetes Insipidus

ChronoCleanse: Detox Your Biological Timeline

The Limb You Hide Is the One That Saves You

Leaves, Bones, and Whisper Spells

The Dinosaur Mindset: Prehistoric Tactics for Modern Wealth

Clawing Back Control: A Bastet Method for Boundaries and Empowerment

Samhain Codes of the Forgotten

Orange Alchemy: The Autumnal Spellbook

Monster Within, Master Without

The Sigil That Sleeps

Hearthcraft: Yule Hearth Sigils and Winter Warmth Spells

Temple of the Purring Moon: Rituals from Bastet's Lineage

When the Earth Remembers Your Footsteps

Food for Mood: Eat to Heal Depression, Not Just Survive It

Witch of the Kudzu Vine: Southern Pagan Wealth Secrets

The Invisible Diagnosis: Advocating for Yourself With DI

The Coffin's Lullaby: Sleep Magick and Nightmares as Portals
Ashes of the Will: Rituals for Erasing the Self
The Fracture Rite: Shattering the Magickal Core
Funeral Candles: The Art of Emo Flame Magick
The Black Grimoire: A Blank Ritual for Writing in Absence
Phantom Thirst: A Halloween Survival Guide for Diabetes Insipidus
The Hollow Crown: Emo Royalty and Magick of the Outcast King
Sandpainting for the Soul
Falling Into Balance: Using the Extra Hour to Recalibrate Life
100 Southern Superstitions That Still Work
The DI Child: A Parent's Guide to Raising Hydrated, Happy Kids
The Jungle of Shame: Escaping the Hidden Lab of Doubt
The Witch's Toast: S'mores Spells and Creepy Confections
The Hoodoo Pantry: Spells from the Mason Jar
The Immortal Fortune: Secret Wealth Lessons from Captain Jack Harkness
The Specter's Embrace: Magick for Channeling Ghostly Lovers
Grateful Waters: A Thanksgiving Survival Guide for Diabetes Insipidus
The Seizure Gospel
Harvestbind: Autumn Sigils and Samhain Spells
Doctor Who: The Algorithmic Awakening
Silent Nights, Steady Waters: A Christmas Survival Guide for Diabetes Insipidus
The Extra Hour Effect: How One Hour Can Transform Everything
Blade Between the Breaths
Running with the Mountain Shadows
Echoes of the Failed Experiment – Becoming a Living Legacy

Swamp Witches & River Ghosts: Real Southern Hauntings

Cornbread Prophecies: Magical Recipes from a Southern Table

Doctor Who: The Signal in the Star

Bloomcraft: Spring Sigils and Equinox Enchantments

Vanisher: How to Disappear from the Internet Without Losing Your Life

The Ultimate Christmas Cookie Cookbook

The Unbreakable Parent: How to Mentally Survive Raising Kids in a Broken World

Time Debt: How to Reclaim the Hours You Didn't Know You Lost

One Month, One Million: Unconventional Cash Creation Tactics

Doctor Who: The Cyber Conversion Protocol

Black Friday Frenzy: The Art of Finding Hidden Online Deals

The Grimoire Buried Under the Apple Tree

Digital Couponing Masterclass: Your Step-by-Step Guide to Black Friday Savings

The Fire Inside the Flint

Shadows on the Ceiling: The Emo Guide to Astral Magick

The Bone-Eaters Beneath Us

Black Friday Bundle Blueprint: Creating Irresistible Product Packages for Maximum Sales

Thirteen Nights of Unbinding

Doctor Who: Engines of Influence

Pumpkin Spice Alchemy: Recipes of Fire and Frost

When Raptor Met Rexy: Prehistoric Lessons in Wild Romance

Oblivion's Candle: Burn the Path Behind You

Campfire Curses and Chocolate: A Halloween S'mores Grimoire

The Wallet That Wasn't Mine: Breaking Free from Inherited Scarcity

The Cola Zodiac: What Your Fizz Says About Your Fate

Frostfire Fortune: Unlocking Winter's Hidden Prosperity

Signal Jamming: Detox Your Brain from Info Overload

The Dust of the Forgotten Rite

The Golden Cat Sigils: Drawing Power in Bastet's Name

Mud Magick: The Prosperity of Getting Dirty

Savory Spicefall: Beyond the Pumpkin Pie

Pumpkin Spice Apothecary Kitchen

The Pumpkin Spice Economy: Turning Trends into Billions

The Ember Veil: 13 Nights of Fire Magick

Financial Freeze: When Earning Triggers Panic

The Gingerbread Alchemist: Sweet Recipes with a Twist

Biosynth Power: Programming Yourself from Scratch

Echoes from the Talking Circle

Truffle Alchemy: Fungus of Fortune

Spores of Power: The Truffle Witch's Handbook

Doctor Who: The Tower That Speaks

The Mycelium Veil: Truffle Magick Unbound

Broke But Ashamed: Healing the Shame Wound of Debt

The Evergreen Mind: Growth Through Winter Stillness

The Black Veil Truffle Rite

The Voice Beneath Symbols

Witchlight on the Bayou: Swamp Spells for Sovereignty

I Grew Up Poor and Now I Sabotage My Success

The Lantern of Hollow Souls

Shutdown Survival: A Citizen's Guide to Thriving When Government Stops

When Abundance Feels Like a Threat: Healing the Hidden Fears of Enough

The Scarecrow Grimoire

Owls of the October Veil

Candlewax and Curses: A Halloween Spellbook

Excavating the Inner Fossil – Transforming Fossilized Thoughtforms into Tools of Power

The Yule Witch's Spellbook: Magick for the Holiday Season

Haunted Christmas: Ghost Stories for Winter Nights

The Christmas Survival Guide: Thriving Through the Chaos

The Bone Orchard Rites

Haunted Commerce: The Ghost in the Marketplace

When Money Triggers the Inner Child

Silent Night with the Silence: A Christmas Thriller

The Lightning Crown: Living and Leading Through Seizures

TARDIS Tidings: Festive Stories from the Whoniverse

Autumn Reset: Slowing Down Without Falling Behind

The Trillion Dollar Soul: Rewriting the Currency of Reality

Truffle Eclipse Magick

Micro-Manifestations: Quick Magick That Works

5-Minute Rituals for Busy Witches

The Marshmallow Massacre: Halloween Treats with a Sinister Twist

Blood and Blackberry Thorns

Magickal Mornings: Rituals for a Blessed Christmas Day

Embers of the All-Hallows Fire

The Pumpkin Market Collapse

The Hour You Gained: Transforming Time Into Power

The Chamber Must Be Sealed: Mastering the Power of Controlled Access

The Cursed Manuscript of Petosiris

The Festive Hearth: Creating Holiday Traditions

Darkness Rising: Thriving as Nights Grow Longer

Harvesting Time: Turning the Year's End Into Your New Beginning

Petosiris and the 13th Zodiac Key

Wagewound: When Paychecks Become Identity Prisons

Walls That Watch

The Silent Feast: Rituals of Power in the Longest Night

The Distortus Legacy : Becoming a Deformed King in a Perfect World

The Hollow Masks

The Gratitude Furnace: Forging Gold from Thanks

Feast of Inner Gold: Eating for Energy and Enlightenment

Haunted Commerce: The Season of Spending Spirits

Fear Bonds: How Panic Creates Profit

Black Friday E-Commerce Playbook: Sales Tactics to Skyrocket Your Holiday Revenue

Budgeting for Black Friday: A Holiday Savings Planner

Haunting the Harvest Moon

The Warrior's Water: Emergency Preparedness for People With DI

The First Sip of the Year: A New Year's Survival Guide for Diabetes Insipidus

Doctor Who: The Thirteenth Node

The Unseen Struggle: Mental Health, Anxiety, and Chronic Thirst

The Hearth's Hidden Ledger: Counting Energies as Currency

The Gift Alchemist: Turning Any Offering Into Gold

The Papyrus of the Bound Spirit

The Magick of Leftovers: Transmutation in the Fridge

Frost and Fortune: Christmas Wealthcraft for the Modern Magus

Last-Minute Gifts: Creative Ideas on a Budget

10 Secrets to Surviving Holiday Crowds

The Witch's Dow Jones

The Witches' Graveyard Shift

Pumpkin Sigils: Carving Rites for Midnight Power

The Secret Shopper's Black Friday Guide: How to Get Early Access and VIP Deals

Fever in the Foundation
The Neuralyzer Reset: Reprogram Your Morning Routine
Lightning Lessons of the White Painted Woman
The Enchanted Snowflake
The Magic Sip: Surviving Disney Parks with Diabetes Insipidus
The One Who Draws Through You
Santa's Secrets: A Magical Holiday Planner
Silent Bells, Loud Miracles: Self-Help for the Season of Stillness
The Sugar Spell Codex: Confectionary Magick of Christmas
Autumn Hexcraft: Fallen Leaves, Fallen Barriers
Sleep Like a Fortress: Build a Life Where Insomnia Can't Survive
Nowhere Was Ever Home
Christmas Under the Stars: A Celestial Holiday Guide
Rentproof: How to Never Be Evicted Again
Workless: Escape the 9-5 Without Being Broke
The Gilded Gift: A Wealth Altar for Christmas Morning
The Black Friday Grimoire
The Hollowing: Ceremonies of Spiritual Collapse
Doctor Who: The Nameless Signal
Where the Eagle Hides His Courage
The Dwarf Tyrant's Ascent: Claiming Power in a World of Giants
The Currency of the Dead: Trading with Spectral Bankers
The Icebound Witch: Survival and Magick in the Cold
The Emergency Money Mind: Constant Crisis, Zero Calm
Thirst & Roses: A Valentine's Survival Guide for Diabetes Insipidus
Springing Into Clarity: Mastering the Energy Shift of Daylight Saving
Speed of the Nanotyrant: Agile Strategies for Life's Hunt

The 90-Day Reset: A Science-Backed Guide to Reinvent Yourself Before the New Year

The Coil of Thorns

Timegates Unleashed

Dopamine Fasting 2.0: Rewiring Your Brain in a World of Overstimulation

The Nanotyrannus Mutation: Embracing Your Differentiated Form

Unwritten January: How to Use the Blank Page of the Year to Re-Author Your Life

Feast of the Forgotten Spirits: Ancestor Magick for the Holidays

The Burnout Codex: A System for Thriving Beyond Stress

I Don't Deserve to Have Money

When the King Doesn't See You: The Shadow Predator's Guide

The Reset Ritual :A Guide to Shedding Last Year's Weight—Emotional and Physical—by Spring Cleaning Your Soul

Calendar Alchemy: Learn to Bend Time and Productivity around Your Natural Rhythms

The Mirror Contract: A One-Sentence Agreement with Yourself that Unlocks Real Change

The Nile Formula: Sacred Flow for Millionaire Minds

Forward Momentum: Productivity Rituals for the Lost Hour

Harvest Gold: Wealth Magick of Pumpkin Spice Commerce

The Magick of Christmas Lights: Illuminating Holiday Rituals

Cranberry Crown: Royal Self-Worth through Ritual Meals

Petosiris and the Worms of the Feathered Throne

The Evergreen Equation: Self-Help for Sustained Growth

The Rain Will Wash Us Away: Emo Weather Magick

Snowlight Shadows: Magick Under Frozen Stars

Doctor Who: Merger of Empires

The Light Within the Feast: Magickal Wealth of Yuletide Flame

Momentum Machines: Small Habits Designed to Snowball into Unstoppable Forward Motion

Calm Spells: Magickal Solutions for Anxiety Relief

Santa's Final List: The Naughty Never Leave

The Mystic's Guide to Banishing Worry

The Silence Dividend: Turning Quiet Mornings into Compounding Growth All Year

Charmed Stillness: Rituals to Ease the Mind

Blood Spiral Ascension

The Vanishing Heart Invocation

Crystal Calm: Harnessing Stones for Anxiety

The Nano Tyrant Code: Strength in the Small Predator

The Energy Ledger: Accounting Methods for Vitality, Not Just Money

Snowglobe Mindset: Shake Up Your Thoughts, Settle Into Peace

The Weight of the Feather: Anubis's Codes for Soul Balance

Pocket Peppermint Power: Tiny Rituals for Big Holiday Energy

Shadowkeeper of the Golden Jackal: Anubis's Path to Energetic Protection

The Witch's Breath: Anxiety Relief Through Magickal Breathing

The Tiny Ember: Pocket Motivation for Cold Days

Stocking Sorcery: Mini Spells for Holiday Luck and Prosperity

Warm Hands, Steady Heart: Micro Grounding for Winter Anxiety

The Jackal's Lantern: Guide-Lights for Walking the Dark Path

Anubis's Silent Steps: Rituals for Stealth, Peace & Emotional Quiet

The Bonewake Protocol

Extinction-Proof: How to Outlive Trends, Trauma, and Time

The Fourth Doctor: The Eccentric Wanderer

The Second Doctor: Chaos and Charm in the TARDIS (Patrick Troughton, 1966–1969)

The Third Doctor: Earthbound Defender of Time (Jon Pertwee, 1970–1974)

The First Doctor: Genesis of the Time Lord (William Hartnell, 1963–1966)

The Fourth Doctor: The Eccentric Wanderer *(Tom Baker, 1974–1981)*

The Fifth Doctor: Elegance and Empathy (Peter Davison, 1982–1984)

The Sixth Doctor: A Kaleidoscope of Conflict (Colin Baker, 1984–1986)

The Seventh Doctor: The Strategist of Shadows (Sylvester McCoy, 1987–1989)

The Eighth Doctor: A Time Lord's Renaissance (Paul McGann, 1996)

The War Doctor: A Time Lord's Burden (John Hurt, 2013)

The Ninth Doctor: The Healer of Worlds *(Christopher Eccleston, 2005)*

The Tenth Doctor: The Lonely Hero (David Tennant, 2005–2010)

The Eleventh Doctor: The Madman in a Box (Matt Smith, 2010–2013)

The Twelfth Doctor: The Rebel with a Cause (Peter Capaldi, 2013–2017)

The Thirteenth Doctor: Breaking the Mold **(Jodie Whittaker, 2017–2022)**

The Fourteenth Doctor: A New Beginning (David Tennant, 2022–2023)

The Fifteenth Doctor: Rewriting the Stars
(Ncuti Gatwa, 2023–2025)

Santa's Shortcut to Success: Micro Habits for a Better New Year

The Midnight Cocoa Manifesto: Comfort Rituals for Hard Nights

Why I Can't Save: Trauma Blocks to Financial Planning

Dino Brain, Mega Goals: Rewire Yourself for Savage Success.

Jurassic Profit: Unearth Your Inner Millionaire Fossil

Scales & Softness: Dating with Dino Heart

Carnotaurus Dreams.

Red Willow Thinking.

Reindeer Resilience: How to Keep Going When You're Exhausted

Candlewick Courage: Lighting Strength in Dark Seasons.

Elf-Mode Focus: Fast Attention Fixes for Busy Seasons

Futureproof Feelings: Emotional Skill-Building for Resilience No Matter What the New Year Brings

The 90-Day Rewire: Transform Your Neural Pathways Before Spring Blooms

Jolly Rich: Christmas Micro-Money Magick for Fast Prosperity.

Gingerbread Gratitude: Mini Practices for a Happier Holiday

Trauma-Spending: When Money Becomes a Drug

Goal Skeletons: Build Minimalist Frameworks for Resolutions That Last

The Snarl Strategy: Growling Back at a World That Silenced You

The Hourglass Reset: Reclaiming What the Clock Took

Yule Claw: Dino Rites of Light in the Darkness

Sacred Circles: Grounding Rituals for Anxious Souls

Clockstopper's Gut: Rebuilding the Core of Time

Winterfire Drive: Harness the Cold Season's Stillness to Ignite Deep Motivation

The 5-Minute Productivity Hack: Small Steps to Big Results

Light Ascending: A Self-Help Guide to Longer Days

Inner Economy: Trade Self-Doubt for Confidence Like a High-Value Currency

Simple Success: Decluttering Your Life for Better Results

The Resilient Mind: Thriving in Tough Times

The 2026 Playbook: Mastering the Year Ahead

The Spring Sleep Solution: Conquering Fatigue After Time Change.

The Hormonal Compass: Navigate Back to Your Youth

Golden Vision: Eating for Your Eye Color with the Power of Ghee

Lionhearted Love: Strength in Relationships

MiB Mindset: Think Like a Cosmic Agent

The Ladder of Small Wins: Climb Out of Stagnation by Stacking Micro-Victories

The Momentum Hour: Gaining More in Less Time.

The Year of You: A Self-Help Blueprint for Unapologetic Self-Ownership

The Dust That Watches You Back.

The Astral Parent

Shadow of the King: The Nanotyrannus Parable

Tiny Tidings of Triumph: Small Wins That Change Your Life

Dwarf Tyrant Rising: When You're the One They Overlook

The Bank Account Mirror: Healing How You See Yourself Through Money

Cretaceous Black

When Love Costs Too Much: Romantic Triggers and Financial Wounds

Dream-Eater's Guide to Wealth

Unzipped Reality: The Jacket That Opens Portals

The Power of No: How to Set Boundaries and Get Rich

Keeper of the Desert Veil: Anubis's Teachings on Illusion & Truth

Redacted Stargates: Stories the SGC Buried

The Clock That Dripped Time

Doctor Who: The Silent Acquisition

Hairline Manifestation: Unlocking Power at the Edge of Thought

Cash-Eater Crickets: How Insects Predict Economic Collapse

Dead Pet Whisperer: Grief Alchemy from the Other Side

The Love Algorithm Is Broken: Hack Romance Before It Hacks You

The Rite of the 8-Limbed Seal

Melt the Moon: A Fire Ritual to Reshape Emotion

Venomous Miracles: Healing Through the Poison Path

Wealth Without Water: The Post-Aquatic Rich Life

The Butterfly Betrayal: When Change Turns on You

The Quiet Upgrade: How Humans Are Secretly Rebuilding Themselves Without Asking Permission

Nobody Taught Us This: The Missing Human Manual for Money, Energy, and Self-Respect

You Were Never Broken: Why Most People Are Reacting Normally to an Unstable World

After the Noise Ends: How Humans Reset When the World Finally Goes Quiet

The Month That Tells the Truth: Why January Reveals What the Rest of the Year Hides

Tremors Party Unleashed: The Ultimate Guide to a Graboids Birthday Bash

Cold Start Human: Rebooting Motivation Without Forcing Momentum

The Year that doesn't start until they say

Love Without Performance: What Connection Looks Like When No One Is Watching

February Is a Mirror: What Love Exposes About You

How We Learned Love Wrong: Uninstalling Cultural Myths About Connection

You Are Not Too Much: Why Needing Love Is Not a Flaw

The Crooked Fence Covenant: Backwoods Boundaries and Witch Wealth

The Day That Keeps Repeating: Why Your Life Feels Stuck—and How to Shift It Gently

Nothing Changes Until Something Softens: Escaping Repetition Without Violence to Yourself

Same Life, Different Ending: How Tiny Choices Rewrite Repetition

The Loop Isn't Punishment: Why You're Being Asked to Learn, Not Suffer

Panic at the Register: Retail Anxiety and Public Shame

The Secret Formula to Becoming an Influencer in 90 Days

The New Rich: How to Retire by 35

Digital Nomad Secrets: How to Travel the World and Make Millions

Burn Your Waiting Room: Escape the Delay Spiral

Strapped for Pleasure: A Complete Guide to Pegging and Strap-On Play

Locked in Desire: A Guide to Chastity Play and Intimate Control

Burrowing into History: Groundhog Day Through the Ages

The Shadow Forecast: The Science of Groundhog Day

Choice Cascades: How One Decision in January Sets Ripples for the Whole Year

The Anti-Anxiety Blueprint: Mastering Fear and Stress for Success

The Ancestral Path of the Jackal Priest

Winterborn Titans: Giants of Ice and Stone

The Extinction Spire

The Emotion That Made Me Millions

Delete Their Voice: Become Unreachable

The Frostbound Mysteries: Mythical Beings of January's Chill

The Roar Within: Unlocking Your Potential

From Burrow to Sky: Groundhog Day Explained

The Boogey Book: Festive Ward-Off Edition

Fooled Ya! The Psychology Behind Great Pranks

April Fools' Alchemy: Transforming Everyday Items into Pranks

Anchor Habits: Root Yourself in Unshakable Routines That Endure Seasonal Change

Emerald Waters: A St. Patrick's Day Survival Guide for Diabetes Insipidus

The Groundhog's Legacy: Myths, Legends, and Facts

Six Weeks of Mystery: The Truth Behind Groundhog Day

The Upgrade Mind: Tech-Like Patches and Updates for Your Mental Operating System

Moon Blood, Star Flesh: Embracing Your Hybrid Nature

Groundhog Lore and Legend: A Complete Guide

You Are the Lie They Can't Kill

Download a Different Reality

The Quiet Advantage: Winning Without Announcing Yourself

A Year of Gratitude: Unlocking Joy

Touch Grass: A Pagan Reset for a Burned-Out Digital World

Cold Start Wealth: Building Financial Power from a Standing Still Point

Astrology Without Fate: Using Cycles Without Surrendering Control

The Future is Remote: Work Less, Earn More, Live Anywhere

Harvest of Silence

The Algorithm Knows Your Name
April Fools' Day for Introverts
Soft Power Systems: Influence That Doesn't Exhaust You
Practical Magick for Real Life: Focus, Intent, and Follow-Through
January Is a Lie: Designing Momentum Without the Calendar
Universal Flow: Managing DI in High-Energy Theme Parks
Electric Allure: Exploring Erotic Electro-Play
The Masked Embrace: Exploring Sensory Deprivation
The Ultimate April Fools' Survival Guide
Splashproof Survival: Waterparks & Wave Pools with DI
Agile Predator, Still King: Crafting Your Speed in a World That Celebrates Size
The Shadow Feast: Groundhog Day's Sinister Side
The Bug's Business Model
Edge of Bliss: Mastering the Art of Tease and Denial
Midnight Alchemy: Rituals for Transformation Between the Old Year and the New
Punxsutawney Bloodlines: A Groundhog Day Horror
The Burrower: Groundhog Day's Darkest Secrets
Buried Alive: A Groundhog Day Horror Story
Blood Moon Markets: The Witch's Guide to Wealth Magick
The Groundhog's Shadow: What It Means for the World
Seasonal Shadows: The Groundhog Day Phenomenon
The Shadow's Curse: A Groundhog Day Horror Tale
Punxsutawney Revealed: A Guide to Groundhog Day
Safari Hydration: Zoo & Wildlife Park Survival for DI
The Foolproof Prank Planner
***Latex Lust: Embracing Fetish Fashion* is a sophisticated**
Whip & Whisper: The Dynamics of Impact Play
The Shadow Burrow Chronicles: Horror Beneath the Ground
Frozen Shadows: A Groundhog Day Thriller
The Groundhog's Revenge: A February Nightmare

Burrow of the Damned
Everyday Enchantment: Magickal Practices for Modern Living
Budget Bliss: The Easy Path to Financial Freedom
Six More Weeks of Terror
The Oxygen Debt
The Ice Veil: Mystical Beasts of January's Shadows
Roots That Remember
Polar Myths: Creatures of the Icy Abyss
The Marginalia Covenant
AI and the Occult: Digital Spirits, Sigils, and Cyber-Witchcraft
Roleplay Realms: Crafting Fantasies and Scenes
The Last Clean River
Lover in the Shadows: A Groundhog Day Tale
Buried Hearts: A Groundhog Day Gothic Romance
Anubis Wept for Petosiris
The Lantern Knows Your Name
Rituals of the Last Shadow
The Bell That Rings for No One
Shadows of Love and Death
The Groundhog's Bride: A Dark Valentine's Tale
Frozen Kisses: A Horror Romance for Groundhog Day
The Creative Spark: Igniting Your Passion Projects
From Cub to King: A Journey of Transformation
Six Weeks to Midnight: A Groundhog Day Romance
Tide of the Unclean
Burrow of Desire: A Groundhog Day Paranormal Romance
The Shadow Magick Almanac: Harnessing Groundhog Day Energies
AI for Emo Influencers: Growing an Online Following Without the Anxiety
AI for the Melancholy Millionaire: Making Money Without Social Interaction

Winter's Grip: A Horror Romance Beneath the Frost
Shadowed Hearts: A Love Buried in Winter's Chill
The Shadow Lover: A Groundhog Day Gothic Love Story
Beneath the Burrow: A Groundhog Day Thriller
The Punxsutawney Conspiracy
The Crimson Pact: Emo Blood Oath Magick
The Shadows of Gallifrey: A Doctor Who Horror Collection
Whispers in the Vortex: Chilling Tales from the TARDIS
AI Ghostwriting for Emo Souls: How to Make Money Writing Without Trying
The Anti-Social Emo's Guide to AI-Powered Freelancing
Emo AI Therapy: Talking to Robots When Humans Suck
Cry & Collect: AI-Powered Passive Income for Emos
The Weeping Angel Chronicles: A Collection of Terror
Dating Without the Mask
The Clockwork Menace: Horror Stories from the Future
Tender Doesn't Mean Weak
Not a Burden, Not a Bonus
Dalek Nightmares: Stories of Ultimate Extermination
The Empty Child's Curse: Tales of Horror and Fear
The TARDIS Ghost Files: Hauntings Across the Universe
Soft Armor, Open Heart
Chosen Gently
Love That Doesn't Rush You
Financial Gaslighting: When You're Made to Feel Crazy About Money.
After the Bees Went Silent
The Soil Knows Your Name
The Quantum Magick Codex: Unlocking the Hidden Laws of Reality
The Gingerbread Golem's Awakening: A Tale of Sweet Revenge

The Gingerbread Golem Chronicles: Guardians of Frost Hollow

The Power of Focus: Eliminate Distractions, Achieve Greatness

Sacred Submission: The Dynamics of D/s Relationships

The Magick of Numbers: Unlocking the Hidden Codes of the Universe

Blood and Bones: The Ancient Magick of Life and Death

Doctor Who: The Collapse Dividend

Thesis of the Unremembered

Desired as You Are

The Energy Budget of Love

Romancing Your Potential: The Love Month Growth Guide

Seen, Not Studied

Screams from the Void: Horror Stories Inspired by Doctor Who

The Silence Is Watching: A Collection of Dread

Under the Floorboards

The House of Feathers and Fangs

Emperor Bones, Hollow Crown

Goreglyphs of the Boiling Deep

The Coven That Screamed Back

The Stacks That Breathe

Love That Adapts

Nightmares on Gallifrey: Frights from the Doctor Who Universe

Apache Ways to Heal Powerfully

Belos Left No Corpses

The Algorithm Hates You (Good.)

Starve the Soul, Feed the Flame

Romance Without Apology

The Carbon Illusion

Your Nervous System is Your GPS

Where Rest Learns Your Name: Six Gentle Bedtime Stories for Minds That Work Differently

Soft Armor for Tender Nights: Six 5-Minute Bedtime Stories for Hearts That Have Been Hurt

Paws of Night, Path of Stars: Six 5-Minute Bedtime Stories Guided by Bastet and Anubis

When the Mind Needs a Lamp: Six 5-Minute Bedtime Stories for Gentle Mental Health Care

Imbolc Roar: Awakening the Dino Flame

The Titan Never Died

Witchflesh Harvest

Become the Thought They Can't Unsee

Golden Threads: The Sensuality of Body Worship

Chains of Desire: Exploring the Beauty of Restraint

Glyphs Written in Organs

Living Below the Line

Palismen Don't Scream—Until They Do

The Boiling Isles Devour the Weak

Hexside Anatomy Lab

Philip Wittebane and the First Body

Money PTSD: When Trauma Hijacks Your Finances

Brother, Bone, and Betrayal

Lipstick Like a Weapon: A Goth Girl's Guide to Emotional Dominance, Boundaries, and Quiet Intimidation

The Scar Is the Portal

Don't Grow—Mutate

Built from Breakdown: The Collapse Code

The Collector's First Lesson

Glyph Failure Syndrome

Philip Wittebane and the Discipline of Lies

The Making of Belos

Flesh Does Not Belong

The Golden Guard Prototypes

Coven Marks as Control Wounds
The Voice Belos Invented
The Boogeyman Within: Shadow Work for Personal Transformation
The Energy Edge: Reclaiming Your Power
Mindful March: A Quick Guide to Intentional Living
Love on Autopilot: Rekindle Your Relationship Instantly
Spring Renewal: Refresh Your Mindset Before the Equinox
Velvet Control: The Subtle Art of Erotic Choking
Erotic Shadows: Playing with Voyeurism and Exhibitionism
The Green Pulse Awakens
Equinox Bones
Immortality Is a Disease
Cold-Blooded Focus
The Invasive Advantage
The Lonely Assassin's Love: A Weeping Angel Romance
Philip Is Still Inside
Become the Signal That Replaces the Noise
When the Soil Says Yes
Shedding What No Longer Protects You
The Shadow Key: Unlocking the Power of Your Dark Self
The Enchanted Chocolate Rituals: Magickal Recipes for Love & Wealth
Love in the Vortex: A Doctor Who Horror Romance
Grimwalker Number Seventeen
The Boy Who Woke Again
Sad Girls Don't Beg: Reclaiming Self-Worth When Melancholy Is Mistaken for Weakness
Raising Pagan Children in a Non-Pagan World
The Pagan Homeschool Exit Strategy
Protecting Childhood While Preparing for Adulthood
Curriculum for the Dead
Too Much for Who? Reclaiming the Power of Intensity

Your Nervous System Is the Algorithm
Memories That Don't Belong to Him
The Golden Guard Template
Time-Locked Hearts: A Gallifreyan Gothic Romance
Ostara's Hatchlings: Fertile Dino Magick
The Dalek's Heart: A Tale of Forbidden Love
The Jackal's Final Game
Where Wild Magic Took My Brother
Where Love Meets Reality
Volume Without Apology
The Mind of Stillness: Petosiris's Hidden Teachings on Power
Doctor Who: The Final Shareholder Meeting
The Archive of Unfinished Lives
AI for Emo Musicians: Automating Your Sad Soundtracks
AI-Generated Emo Art: Selling Melancholy in Digital Form
Ashes Where the Cathedral Slept
The Monarch of Splintered Wings
People-Pleasing Is a Survival Strategy Past Its Expiration Date
Velvet Carnage Covenant
The Intensity Advantage
Attention Is a Finite Resource—You're Overspending It
Emotional Debt Compounds Faster Than Money
The Siege of Thornlit Graves
When the Bone King Wept Black
Comfort Is the Most Expensive Addiction
The AI Gothpreneur: Building a Business Without Any Social Interaction
AI & Tarot: Emo Divination for the Digital Age
Sad AI Aesthetics: Emo Branding & Personal Style
Black Sails Over a Dying Sun
The Crimson Parliament of Wolves
Cathedral of Veins and Thunder
The Orchard of Hanging Saints

The Self-Discovery Path: Find Your True Purpose You Were Taught to Self-Sabotage Politely

www.ingramcontent.com/pod-product-compliance
Lightning Source LLC
LaVergne TN
LVHW022223200926
848481LV00006B/2099